Iconic Restaurants
OF
ST. LOUIS

Iconic Restaurants
OF
ST. LOUIS

ANN LEMONS POLLACK

AMERICAN PALATE

Published by American Palate
A Division of The History Press
Charleston, SC
www.historypress.com

Front cover, top left: courtesy of the author; *top right*: courtesy of the author; *bottom left*: courtesy of the National Museum of Transportation; *bottom right*: courtesy of the author.
Back cover: Missouri Historical Society, Photographs and Prints Collection.

Unless otherwise noted, all images are courtesy of the author.

First published 2020

Manufactured in the United States

ISBN 9781467145121

Library of Congress Control Number: 2020941808

For all the ones I've fed before.

Contents

Contents

Acknowledgements

*I*conic Restaurants of St. Louis is a labor of love. Make no mistake, it was definitely labor. The encouragement of my family and friends, offers of art from two gifted women and the assistance of many professionals from the hospitality industry made it all possible.

The dedication of this book, which is to the people I've fed, begins, of course, with my family. There is no question that I need to offer gratitude to my children, who support me as much (or more) as I have supported them. Terry and Jennifer Lemons, Wendy Pollack and Dara Pollack Silverberg and their spouses and partners, Jane, Lamar and Eric, have been patient with both my elated raves and grumbling conversations. The next generation, Ben, Sarah, David, Mattye, Tom Even, Hanne Elise, Elaine and Aliyah, and their partners and offspring make me smile, especially when I watch them at table (or other locations of being nourished, referring to our newest, Emberly). And a happy flap of the flour-crusted apron to my cousin Dawn Lockwood, always ready to talk food, especially baking.

My best friend from our days in nursing school, Mary Mallory, "Auntie" to the next generations, is always there for me. Her Majesty Sally I, Potato Queen and Duchess of Escargot and her consort, Mr. T, Esq., are valuable resources, well beyond being brunch mates. Old pals Ron, Bill and Gerry have been happy to be fed and to talk about food and everything else, including having my back when I was beating my head against the wall.

Founder and proprietor of Annie Gunn's, Thom Sehnert, searched high and low for a photo of his flood-inundated restaurant. I regret that technical problems with reproduction kept us from using it, but Thom and his two resident wine geeks, Glenn Bardgett and John Cain, were full of good suggestions. Father and son Michael and Paul Beffa, who closed their old place and then reopened Beffa's with even more hours and more choices, gave me a warm welcome. Blueberry Hill's Joe Edwards was happy to offer assistance and turned me over to his daughter Hope Edwards for some technical help with artwork. At Chuck-A-Burger, Ron Stille told great stories with much laughter. Jim Fiala, who first spied us as he peered out from a kitchen in Manhattan, allowed me good access to the restaurant on a day with the light just right and answered many questions. Cake queen Lia Weber, formerly of Hendel's and TLC's *Next Great Baker*, gave me plenty of info. Charlie Gitto is always fun to talk to and to pass on a story or two. Ellen Cusumano shared photos with me and talked about her grandparents who started Kemoll's.

Qui Tran patiently answered my questions about his family's Mai Lee. Life within a delicatessen was what Alan Protzel talked about when I called him. The store was founded by his father, was owned by his late brother and him and is now run by his son. Alan Buxbaum answered some of my questions about Rizzo's Top of the Tower. Don Casalone has an apparently bottomless supply of old ads, which he's been generous enough to allow use of. One of the founders of Schlafly, the St. Louis Brewery and the Tap Room, Dan Kopman, as usual, was a font of knowledge, dates and proper spellings. From Sidney Street Cafe, Chris Nashan updated me on several things. Jeanne Venn, concierge extraordinaire at the Chase Park Plaza, told great stories about the Tenderloin Room, but, as is the nature of her profession, discreetly left other tales pretty much alone. Stories of Tony's restaurant, especially in its early days, came from Tony Bommarito; James Bommarito gave some of his valuable time to give me updates on their pending move. Trattoria Marcella's Steve Kormorek was kind enough to talk about how it all evolved and about a few of his customers. Anent St. Louis Union Station, Nancy Milton led the way and brought me to Darlene Menietti, the unofficial resident historian of the historic building. Further assistance with images came from Teresa Militello and Charles Taylor with the National Museum of Transportation. At the Missouri History Museum, Lauren Salwasser helped me through the maze. Larry Giles, creator of the National Building Arts Center, dug out a fine piece of Vitrolite from the now-gone Pope's Cafeteria downtown on Washington Avenue for me to photograph.

Who would have thought to find a photograph of Mammer Jammer in a gallery in Carmel, California? Robin Winfield had a fine one and gave me permission to use it. And Marilynne Bradley, the St. Louis queen of watercolor, always a help, gave permission to use her Schneithorst's painting.

I'm happy to give a final tip of the hat to Greg and Ann Rhomberg, whose enthusiasm and support for St. Louis nostalgia is nothing short of remarkable.

And, as will always be, to Joe.

Merci beaucoup, as our founding mother, Madame Laclede, would have said, to all.

Introduction

What is an iconic restaurant? This book is the offshoot of my previous one, *Lost Restaurants of St. Louis.* As I wrote the latter book, at my publisher's preference, I discussed only a few of the great restaurants of St. Louis that were still in existence. So, when The History Press approached me to do a second book as part of its Iconic Restaurants series, it seemed like the logical next step.

What makes a restaurant iconic? The term *icon* has another meaning, of course, beyond that for religious images (the original use of the word) and those wee computer images we're urged to click on. It comes to us from the Greek word *eikenai*, meaning "to seem or be like." I'm happy to use the definition "an emblem or representative symbol."

Many of the eating spots in the previous book were indeed iconic, like Tony Faust's and the Parkmoor, of course. But here was a chance to examine other places St. Louisans remember and, in many cases, can return to. Not all of the restaurants I include here are open, to be sure, but the great majority are.

As I look at the group, one theme stands out. These are stories about families—families working hard, working together, not only to make a living but also to share with their community. In many cases, it's the American dream personified. Make no mistake, this is hard work, from coming up with the capital necessary for opening the doors to showing up early every day. "Owners," said my late husband, Joe Pollack, for many years the restaurant critic at the *St. Louis Post-Dispatch*, "have to be able to do everything. You can't ask the chef to wash the dishes."

These are not restaurant reviews. They're histories and stories about places where St. Louisans have, or had, a good time. One establishment is in a building so old that it hosted a banquet for the Marquis de Lafayette. (He apparently enjoyed himself a great deal.) Another story is about a 1954 cooking demonstration about "Italian meat tubes" by one of the owners, who'd had them in Milan, got a recipe and added them to the menu under their proper name, cannelloni. When two teenaged boys took over their family restaurant, what were the results? Definitely not a disaster. Then there is the tale of a restaurant owner, a nearby business, a rooftop and some eggs.

To my delight, one restaurant appears in both books. Beffa's has, phoenix-like, risen from *Lost Restaurants* and is just reopening with a new generation of Beffas. That two-headed Roman god, Janus, looking to the past and looking to the future, ends and beginnings, should be on the logo.

There are also more than a dozen recipes from the included restaurants. They range from fairly simple dishes to a very involved one that's an example of how today's fine-dining kitchens have to work. Like the recipes in the earlier book, I haven't tested these myself.

There's a happy range of experiences here. These are all Missouri restaurants, but there's an attempt to be geographically diverse. They vary in size from barely holes-in-the-wall to large and, in one case, multiple locations. Some have gone through multiple owners, and others are still in the hands of the founding family. Cuisine ranges across continents, and so do the costs of meals.

I hope that ten years from now we'll have even more iconic restaurants to represent the diversity we are creating and the food and hospitality we're enjoying. But here are places worth exploring.

PART I

ST. LOUIS RESTAURANTS

Annie Gunn's

When Annie Gunn's opened in August 1990, the *St. Louis Post-Dispatch* story led with the fact that this was an Irish pub with a fax machine. They've come a long way since then.

Thom and Jane Sehnert ran the Smoke House Market next door after taking it over from Jane's father, Frank Wiegand, in 1981. The Market dates to 1937, when Andy Kroeger opened it; Frank Wiegand bought an interest in 1951. The building was then an endearingly named rural tavern, the Pot Roast Inn. Thom decided that he would build on the lunch business that the Market's deli sandwiches and picnic tables had created, naming the pub after his grandmother.

It didn't take long for the interior, properly pub-like with hunting prints and lots of dark wood, to get busy. There was even a snug, the small walled-off area seating maybe seven people sometimes found in Irish pubs. The Market, which had long made its own sausages, bacon and ham, along with the rest of its meat counter, gave the kitchen lots of options. Lunch got plenty of business types, and the food went far beyond sandwiches. West County had clearly been waiting for something like this. Dinner reservations were a hot property. Things hummed along.

And then the water came. The Chesterfield Valley, where Annie Gunn's is located, is protected from the nearby Missouri River—at least most of the time—by the Monarch Levee, something almost no one had heard of until the morning of August 1, 1993. The day before, people learned, the levee had been breached by the flooding Missouri. Water poured in, eight

Annie Gunn's during the flood of 1993. *Courtesy of Thom Sehnert.*

to fifteen feet high, covering more than six square miles. Just two weeks before, the Sehnerts had paid off the bank note on the restaurant, seven years early. Now, a news helicopter showed Thom being airlifted off the roof of the building.

Despite an extremely wet autumn, the restaurant reopened in seven months. Not only had it expanded, the Sehnerts also hired a new chef. Lou Rook III rolled into the kitchen.

The food has been described as being at the corner of upscale and home cooking. Increasing amounts of local material are coming out of the kitchen, from summer tomatoes—some of which grow on Thom and Jane's home property—to lamb and cheese and wine. The menu continues to show Rook's fondness for potatoes, although not quite so much as in earlier times; the *Post-Dispatch* critic once asked for, and received, a platter with the eleven different potato dishes being offered that week. The recipe for one of their most popular potato options, a sort of au gratin, is in the back of this book.

There's a wide range of choices, from four burger options and house-made smoked and fried bologna sliders with mustard aioli to at least four different steaks, lamb and pork chops, perhaps some quail and an excellent rendition of calves' liver. The dessert of choice is probably the bread pudding with a

The jeroboam of Graham's tawny port.

banana bourbon sauce. Chef Lou's sous-chef, by the way, is his father, Lou Jr., known to all as "Pappa Lou."

Annie Gunn's is still very casual, but don't let that fool you into thinking you can't get a glass of truly good wine there. Glenn Bardgett has run the wine program since 2001, and his approach is simple. "I want wine that tastes good, that's all." There are about forty wines available by the glass, from a cellar that holds more than nine hundred varieties. Glenn and/or the sommelier John Cain are always around to explain or advise or just to talk about wine. They can also answer why one of the dessert beverage options, a twenty-year-old Graham's tawny port, will come from a jeroboam, one of those wine bottles that holds almost five quarts.

It remains busy after all these years, through water and wine. The snug remains. One employee noted, "There are always people waiting to get in when we unlock the doors in the morning. It's pretty satisfying."

16806 Chesterfield Airport Road, Chesterfield
636-532-7684
anniegunns.com

Beffa's

Rising from the figurative ashes, to the surprise of many, back comes Beffa's. In *Lost Tables of St. Louis*, the story of Beffa Brothers was told, two Swiss brothers who served alcohol and food from 1898. There's an ancient photo on the restaurant's website of Beffa Bros. Place, a pretty casual name for a couple of Swiss from a country where propriety is nearly a religion. Their heirs picked up the mantle of the place near the riverfront and, by 1966, were close to the corner of Olive and Jefferson.

By that time, the establishment had transitioned to a short cafeteria line with sandwiches with meat carved to order and daily specials. It was a bar, of course, but it wasn't so much a drinking spot as a place to congregate. After one move or another, the name of the place never got displayed, so it became, in effect, one of the first underground restaurants, in the modern sense of the word.

That's not to say it was snooty. Plumber's helpers and delivery drivers would be in line with movers and shakers. There were lots of lawyers and politicians, arts types and media people, plus office clerks and cops. It was the original mixed bag. Plenty of tales are told about who was there and what came out of which famous face running into which insider.

Then, zap! Out of the blue, more or less, the place shut down in 2016. Michael Beffa decided to retire.

But in late 2019, rumors rumbled. Finally, word came down: Yes, Beffa's was reopening. Paul Beffa, Michael's son, was taking the helm. As we write, it has just reopened. The cafeteria line is still there, as are most of the daily

Action at the reborn Beffa's.

specials, but the place is going a little more upmarket with dinner. (There's a fine variation on a Cuban sandwich called Three Pigs for those who dig swine.) Also on tap is a Saturday brunch.

They've gotten the band back together, gang. But there's still no sign on the door. (There's also an entrance on Beaumont, the side street.)

Beffa's Bar & Restaurant
2700 Olive Street, St. Louis
beffas.com

Blueberry Hill

Blueberry Hill is a playground for grownups, and we say that in the most admiring way. Joe Edwards's bar and restaurant sits in the Loop neighborhood on the city line between St. Louis and University City. A few blocks north of Washington University, it opened in 1972 and originally was a bar with beer, packaged chips and nuts. And, oh, yes, a hot dog machine, Edwards reports.

He wasn't, he says, very tolerant of serious rowdiness. The blacklisting of overexuberant patrons had a serious effect on profits, and the place nearly closed a couple of times. The biggest feature early on was a jukebox with Edwards's large collection of records. He rotated the records in the jukebox every two weeks, except for one permanent holding, Fats Domino's "Blueberry Hill." He was a big fan of rock 'n' roll; in fact, in 1974, Edwards published *Top 10s & Trivia of Rock & Roll and Rhythm & Blues, 1950–1973*, so detailed that it came in at more than six hundred pages. The music seemed to draw patrons; John Goodman said he and his pals used to come up from suburban Affton as often as they could to pour quarters into the old Seeburg machine.

Joe had been a collector since he was a kid, and his treasures were a theme at Blueberry Hill from the very start. Comic books, records, baseball cards, Pez dispensers, lunchboxes and posters all ended up in cases or on the walls.

Another draw was the dart board, put in at the urging of a patron. Despite the seeming danger of darts combined with beer, it became a regular thing, and over the years, the restaurant fielded a competitive team that saw plenty of coverage in the local sports pages.

The neon sign of Blueberry Hill sets the mood. *Courtesy of Hope Edwards.*

All of this was being accomplished with 3.2 percent beer, the most the University City council would allow. Two years after Blueberry Hill's opening, the city agreed to license the place for 5 percent beer, and a grill was added for hamburgers and such.

The collections, from Howdy Doody to space-related memorabilia, continued to grow and be displayed. Into the mishmash of decor came a collection of pinball machines to add to the diversions. A writer in the *Post-Dispatch* in 1976 described the establishment as "a live museum for war babies," referring to the generation that preceded baby boomers.

Music that wasn't prerecorded arrived in 1985, as the restaurant expanded to both the east and west. Joe had become pals with the legendary rock 'n' roll musician Chuck Berry, who always remained a local resident, and Berry would sometimes do a set or two on the premises. That occasioned a major remodel in 1997. A hole was cut in the bottom of what was known as the Piano Room, a Bobcat was lowered in and the basement dug out even further. They dropped the floor another five feet to make the Duck Room, named for Berry's trademark move. Chuck Berry became a regular for many years, racking up more than two hundred performances, although he explained, "I don't come here for the music, I come here for the wings."

The corner window on the east end regularly draws crowds for its displays. Joe's former wife, Linda, creates wonderful, witty works of art. Twice a year, on the anniversaries of Elvis Presley's birth and death, there are Elvis-themed exhibits with an Elvis impersonator and sometimes other members of his family, as well as celebrations in-house. St. Patrick's Day is feted with something like Patty O'Furniture. Pay attention to the smaller details in such windows. For example, one Halloween window that featured witches had cigarettes strewn about. The brand? Salem.

Having lunch or dinner in a place that resembles the Smithsonian of many people's childhoods is an experience. Weekends draw lots of family groups, although it's hard to tell if twenty-first-century kids think all this stuff is worth the adults' delight. Hearing Uncle Jerry gasp, "I had that lunch

A little bit of almost everything at Blueberry Hill.

box when I was in the second grade at Emerson School" may or may not amuse them. But the crowd is always very mixed, at least until mid-evening. The rule after 9:00 p.m. is over-twenty-one only, something Joe Edwards says he imposed early on after seeing a woman playing pinball at midnight, a cigarette hanging out of her mouth and a six-week-old baby in one arm.

Blueberry Hill is a serious hamburger house, always in contention for best burger in town in the fat hamburger category (as opposed to the flat-grilled division). It's no surprise, considering the neighborhood, that there are several vegetarian and vegan options, and gluten-free items are noted. Lots of beer is on tap, and there's a cider, plus plenty more in cans. Sadly, Joe's Rock 'n' Roll Beer, which was made for Edwards by Dixie Brewery in New Orleans, is no more.

With all the varieties of pop culture on hand, there may be no bigger deal—even more amazing than the Howdy Doody collection—than one particular mention of the house in print. Blueberry Hill made it into a comic book. *Archie's Pals and Gals* featured the restaurant and its proprietor in a 1989 issue as the ageless teen Archie Andrews thinks he's discovered his beloved jalopy parked in front of 6504 Delmar. It's the ultimate compliment for this unique piece of Americana.

Blueberry Hill
6504 Delmar Boulevard, University City
314-727-4444
blueberryhill.com

Broadway Oyster Bar

One of the oldest buildings in St. Louis contains a one-of-a-kind bar/restaurant. The Broadway Oyster Bar sits patiently on South Broadway, a few blocks below Busch Stadium, its flow of customers unchanged despite the opening of Ballpark Village. This is a very different experience. The building dates to at least the 1840s and, by some reports, the 1820s. And it shows it, which is part of the fun.

There are two narrow rooms: the front bar, with a tiny fireplace that's surely original; and the dining room in back, with a view of the kitchen. The rooms are hung with a hodgepodge of items, the kind of assortment that chain restaurants try (in vain) to imitate—posters, stuffed fish, a New Orleans bakery box that decades ago held a king cake. Before this iteration, the building has been a private home, a boardinghouse, a Chinese laundry, a brothel and a record store. If walls could talk, indeed. On the south side is a large patio and covered performance area. Another room has been opened on the north side.

The restaurant appears to have begun in 1979, when Bob Burkhardt and his sister Bonnie opened it primarily as a music club. Burkhardt had a background in clubs, including BB's up the street. Three years later, when it was describing itself as "the last hippie bar in the city," Dennis Connolly and Donna Jeanne Heseman, who worked there, bought the business.

There was always music in the bar, despite its very limited size. Musicians worked in the front by the front door, which was so drafty that a quilt, and eventually a piece of carpet, was tacked up in a vain attempt to alleviate,

Left: A quiet moment at the ancient Broadway Oyster Bar.

Below: The fun starts in the parking lot behind the Broadway Oyster Bar.

ever so slightly, drafts. The music leaned toward bluesy stuff, and over the years, many familiar names have shown up, especially early in their careers.

Connolly put a great deal of focus on the kitchen. There had always been oysters and other seafood, but thanks to Paul Prudhomme, America became very aware of the food of southern Louisiana, both Creole and Cajun, long before most of us even knew there was a difference. Various preparations of Gulf oysters, from raw to Rockefeller, as well as gumbo and jambalaya, took pride of place on the menu. Shrimp and grits, crawfish and, of course, bread pudding were on offer.

Interestingly, there were not only po'boy sandwiches, but grinders as well. Those torpedo-shaped sandwiches go by different names in different parts of the country, like heroes and subs, but it's unusual to have both names on a single menu. In the case of the Broadway Oyster Bar, the po'boys were served in the classic New Orleans style, with fried seafood and dressed, as New Orleanians say, with lettuce, tomato and "mynez" (the Crescent City pronunciation of "mayonnaise"). The grinders—the name is primarily used in southern New England, Connecticut, Rhode Island and western Massachusetts—were made with the same bread, often brought in from traditional New Orleans bakeries like Leidenheimer's and Gendusa's but hollowed out a little. The seafood of choice, not breaded, was sauteed in garlicky butter with green onions and tipped into the bread, along with the pan juices. The oyster ones in particular were a singular delight.

It would be easy to think this was a party bar if the food weren't so good. There's music every night and on weekend afternoons, some bands playing without a cover charge. Every Monday night is a jam session, said to be the longest-running regular jam in the country. During Mardi Gras, which is a big deal in this part of town—the northern edge of the Soulard neighborhood, Mardi Gras Central for St. Louis—things really jump. The patio is covered, and transparent side curtains are put into use on chilly or rainy days, so there's a lot of activity out there.

"Leave Your Attitude at Home" is the slogan on T-shirts and on the huge mural overlooking the parking lot. You may as well; you won't need it. Everyone, including the staff, is here for customers to have a good time.

Broadway Oyster Bar
736 South Broadway, St. Louis
314-621-8811
broadwayoysterbar.com

Café Natasha

Within living memory, but just barely, downtown St. Louis was filled with hordes of office workers. Some of the buildings housed a single company. Others, like the Arcade Building and the Paul Brown Building, held multiple small businesses and practices. Dentist offices, watch repair shops, title companies—the list went on and on. In the Paul Brown Building, which was, in one section, sixteen stories tall, one can imagine what the population was during the workday.

In the words of the old Checkers commercial, "you gotta eat." Downtown was crawling with spots to have lunch. Not all of them were visible to passersby. On the ground floor of the Brown Building there was a passageway, an arcade, that went from Olive Street through to Pine Street. Along the corridor were, among other small businesses, three restaurants. One of them was a tiny café serving breakfast and lunch called the Little Kitchen.

Hamishe Bahrami was educated as a nurse in Iran. Behshid Bahrami was a geologist who was in St. Louis to work for an engineering firm. Originally, he'd come to the States to get his graduate degree. She was going to school and working in New Jersey, where she'd landed. Behshid was her roommate's classmate's brother-in-law. He wooed her with food, they married and she came to St. Louis.

A month before Natasha was born, Behshid was laid off. Behshid, too, was Iranian, and his nationality was an obstacle just getting interviews in the years after the Iranian Revolution and subsequent hostage event. He struggled for more than a year before they took the leap of opening a restaurant. The Little

Kitchen served American things like roast beef sandwiches and homemade pie from Hamishe, as well as Persian food. Persia, of course, is the old name for Iran—probably more romantic and certainly less controversial.

Practically no one in St. Louis knew about Persian cuisine, and the Bahramis didn't know about St. Louis eating habits, but both sides caught on quickly. Business dropped off on Fridays for several weeks in the spring, Hamishe remembers. She asked a friend about it, and the friend explained Lenten rules for Catholics. A fish dish immediately appeared alongside their rice seasoned with dill, which, they found, didn't get completely eaten. A customer said, "Fish with *rice*? You need spaghetti with fish." So they added spaghetti to the plate, with a sauce learned from a New Jersey Italian. Eventually, people stopped eating the spaghetti and scarfed down the rice. Entertainment at the little kitchen was provided by tiny Natasha in a swinging cradle Behshid had built.

They soon opened Café Natasha, dinner only, plus Sunday brunch, in the Delmar Loop. The menu was very small at first but soon grew with things like kebabs and lamb chops. Lots of vegetarian options showed up, especially in the first courses.

Behshid was driven to perfection when it came to food. He told about making osh, a traditional Persian soup. When they began, he said, he used the juice from the roast beef they made for sandwiches at the Little Kitchen for soup. When they closed the Little Kitchen, roast beef was no longer made. The osh became vegetarian, and that was a big hit. Then he began pondering how he could make it vegan, as he sauteed onions in butter for it. That problem, too, he overcame. That's how it went with him, from marinades for each kind of kebab to the best recipe for felafel. He would tinker for months or years.

In 2001, they added Kebab International on South Grand and eventually closed the Delmar spot to combine the two restaurants. Natasha Bahrami, now grown, had come home to help run the restaurant. Behshid Bahrami was a near-constant presence in the house. Customers talk about how he would urge them to pick up the lamb chops with their fingers to get every last succulent morsel of flesh. Hamishe continued in the kitchen and with her baking. The food is no longer only traditional Persian. There are riffs in all directions, like a curry-mustard sauce on tender sliced beef.

In 2014, Natasha established the Gin Room, using the bar of the restaurant and adding a large variety of gins and making her own tonics. She has received national attention for it. Drinkers can order off the same menu; diners can have their gin and their lamb chops, too.

Sadly, Behshid Bahrami died in 2016, but the hospitality remains warm and the menu intriguing. Both Natasha and her mother say they can hear him saying emphatically, "It has to *taste*" as they work in the kitchen.

Café Natasha/The Gin Room
3200 South Grand Boulevard, St. Louis
314-771-3411
cafenatasha.com

Cardwell's

It was a restaurant chain that brought Bill Cardwell to St. Louis. The Gilbert/Robinson group had already opened a Fedora's in Country Club Plaza in Kansas City, where they were based, and then a second one in Washington, D.C. The third, opened in 1984, was in the prime corner on the Midway in the newly reopened Union Station here. Bill Cardwell was the culinary director.

Cardwell's family owned an inn in Vermont. He attended the Culinary Institute of America, arguably the Harvard of culinary schools, especially then. Fedora's was suspiciously close to what was beginning to be called Modern American cuisine. No matter what flag it was flying under, it frequently was very good indeed. Rich Gorczyca, a local guy who'd come to G/R from the Hulling-Apted family's restaurants, was running it. The two men must have gotten along really well, because they decided to strike out on their own.

Together with David Wilhelm of the Forsyth Group, they opened Cardwell's at the southwest corner of Maryland Avenue and Brentwood Boulevard. With three partners, how did they end up naming it Cardwell's? Gorczyca said, "It was easier to spell or pronounce than Wilhelm or Gorczyca."

This was, unquestionably, Modern American cuisine. That was a real change for Clayton, whose successful restaurants had been steakhouses or Italian or French places. The interior felt as though it could have been lifted from a hot restaurant in San Francisco, with a wildly busy bar resting on black-and-white tile floors, dining rooms with dark wood and ultra-white walls with trees here and there. The art caused so much comment and inquiry that the owners had a sheet made up explaining each work.

Claytonians instantly decided they loved what the house was dishing up. So did mobs of other restaurant-goers. And it stayed very busy; there was no sophomore slump. Bill Cardwell was putting out things like a buffalo strip steak with sweet potato hash browns and roast lamb (almost never seen on St. Louis menus) with a shiitake mushroom and potato cake. The sides were as interesting as the mains.

In 1993, rumors began to float through the community. Was Cardwell's contemplating a move? What was going on? It turned out that an expansion was afoot. In the spring of 1994, the owners signed a lease with Plaza Frontenac for a space next to Neiman Marcus. In a shopping center? Cardwell's?

It turned out to be a smart move. The affluent suburb of Frontenac and the surrounding area held plenty of potential diners. The parking was plentiful and there was space for outside dining. And the new digs had several large alcoves, perfect for a little more privacy for, say, a business meal, while not feeling cut off from the excitement of the main dining room. Guests could enter from the mall or from the parking lot.

The menu felt a little more casual than that of the Clayton location. Bill Cardwell, known as a demanding chef, hired the best for his restaurants, both in the kitchen and in the front of the house. The chef whom he took for the new location was Dave Owens. Owens was, and is, a vegetarian, but that didn't inhibit his cooking at all. He was one of a long line of accomplished chefs to pass through that kitchen. Cardwell's serving staff was first-rate, with the occasional exception of the elegant young women at the front of the house who couldn't resist a disdainful glance at a patron who didn't meet their mysterious standards.

The same year, Bill got national notice when Marcel Desaulniers, a big-deal chef with several books to his credit, did one titled *The Burger Meisters*. Bill was one of the featured chefs, and the book won a James Beard Award. Thereafter, his Burger Meister burger was never off the menu.

The Plaza Frontenac Cinema opened in 1998. The idea of being able to eat a meal like that after a movie was almost revolutionary, but soon enough, the flow was enough to warrant the restaurant staying open a little later than it might ordinarily have. That same year, Cardwell and Gorczyca parted ways, with Rich keeping his interest in the Clayton store and Bill taking over Frontenac.

Things never really slowed down. Tables were always in demand, although walk-ins usually could be accommodated. However, the lease on the space was up in 2018, and the owners of the mall offered only a ten-year renewal. Bill Cardwell decided to close up shop. He gave plenty of time for his staff to get jobs elsewhere and for loyal customers to come for one last Chinese barbecued chicken salad (the recipe is in the back of this book) or plate of profiteroles.

Cardwell now is catering, teaching and having a good time. Goodness knows, he's given St. Louis plenty of good times.

Carl's Drive-In

Burgers and root beer made Carl's Drive-In. Things are done the way they've been done for decades at the tiny spot that began life as a service station just after World War I. That morphed into a hot dog stand in 1943, just as World War II's rationing of meat began. But, somehow, the Foot Long Hot Dog Company survived, and in 1950, it was sold to Walter Breeden.

The year 1959 proved to be a pivotal one for the building. In the early hours of February 10, the building sustained considerable damage from a tornado, the one that went on to down the KTVI tower, take a large part of the roof off the Arena and kill eleven people in the area that would be called Gaslight Square. Breeden rebuilt but later that year sold the business to Carl and Pat Meyer. They brought in curb service and a walk-up window. Breeden had been serving IBC Root Beer, and the Meyers, who renamed it Carl's Drive-In, kept their relationship with the brand. IBC had come into being about the time the hot dog stand opened, as St. Louis's Griesedieck family created it to offset the effects of Prohibition.

In 1962, the building was expanded to offer two indoor seating areas. Air conditioning was installed, a good idea, as the grill was within not more than a dozen feet of most of the seats. Things were buzzing, including plenty of teenagers from farther up High School Drive, the restaurant's cross street on Manchester and the street where Brentwood High School stands. The carhops were discontinued—eighty-sixed, as the restaurant slang goes—in 1969.

Frank Cunetto, a previous owner of Carl's Drive-In, works the flattop grill.

But dark clouds were gathering. The IBC supply was endangered. By this time, IBC belonged to Bud Taylor, who began the Chuck-A-Burger stands and ran a root beer concession in Forest Park. Carl was buying the syrup for the drink from him. Taylor went out of the root-beer business in 1975 but passed the formula on to Carl. The big wooden keg was, and still is, right in the middle of the action and to this day rocks and root-beers on with

The specialty of the house at Carl's Drive-In.

the beverage made in-house. (The brand itself was revived and currently belongs to Schweppes Inc.)

The business again changed hands, this time without a name change, when Frank Cunetto bought, first, half the business, and then a year or so later, in 1987, the whole thing. Frank's the guy many of us remember at the grill, slapping the burgers down on the grill to get them cooked with the perfect crispy edges.

What does a diner see—and get— at Carl's Drive In? It's an authentic throwback. Two entrances on opposite sides of the building open onto identical counters with eight stools each. People wait patiently for stools to open up, and the veteran staff sometimes takes orders before those folks sit down. Sometimes, not all of a group can be seated; it's not uncommon when things are busy to see root beers balanced on windowsills and moms or dads eating standing up. The menu is on the back wall, but most folks know what they want. These are flat-grilled hamburgers, with the double arguably giving the best ratio of meat to bun. Frank always understood that getting the burgers in front of customers while still hot was key to their excellence; it's one reason, he says, that he never enlarged things. Toppings have to be specified, to the amazement of young ones who've never had a burger that wasn't from a fast-food place. Another popular item with the young is the Curly-Q dog, carefully slashed so it curls up on a round bun. But it's a long way behind the burgers. And there is the root beer, of course, in properly frosty mugs—unless it's so busy that the mugs don't have enough time to freeze after being washed from the early crowd. The insider's secret here are the shakes, with ice cream scooped out by hand and mixed to order, rich and satisfying. Warning: One of these with two double hamburgers will necessitate an afternoon nap. One more below-the-radar local treat is available here: Ronnie's Rocky Mountain. It's like a Drumstick that's had growth hormones—the very good ice cream from local brand Quezel and plenty of chopped salted peanuts embedded in dark chocolate.

It's not unusual to see famous local faces here—Jack Buck was a regular—and folks home for holiday visits introducing new spouses or out-of-town grandkids to the place. Speculating on which side will have shorter wait times has always been part of the fun.

Frank handed Carl's off to Mike Franklin in 2015, who has promised to continue things. It's still cash only. Long may they grill.

Carl's Drive-In
9903 Manchester Road, Brentwood
314-961-9652
carlsdrivein.com

Casa Gallardo

For some people, the name "Casa Gallardo" evokes a national chain of Mexican restaurants, most of them located conveniently close to an interstate exit in a comfortable suburb. But it began with an idea from a St. Louisan. Ramon Gallardo wasn't born here. He chose St. Louis as his home after deciding not to go to law school in Mexico City, immigrating to Chicago and then moving to St. Louis. He was still very young but soon was working for Stephen J. Apted, whose mother had founded Miss Hulling's. The younger Apted expanded his family's restaurant empire considerably and realized that Gallardo was smart and hardworking. Eventually, Gallardo took over the Apted family's Mexican restaurant downtown, La Sala, and reworked the menu there. It was a success.

But in the tradition of dreaming immigrants, he had bigger things on his mind. He managed a Small Business Loan and opened Casa Gallardo in Westport Plaza in 1975. Everything on the menu was fresh, going beyond the very basic things St. Louis had been offered in Mexican restaurants to that point. And it was *real*.

"I used to say the only thing American was the cash register," said Gallardo. He brought decorative items back in his car when he visited Mexico. He had live music. Instead of hamburger in dishes, he used chopped beef. And he very quickly had a success in the brightly colored, vivacious restaurant. It was hot for date nights and happy hours, thronged on weekends. Westport was a very happening place in those days, with clubs and restaurants and retail establishments, and Casa Gallardo, located on one of the main corridors, was impossible to miss.

It was so successful that within three years, General Mills was pestering him to buy the concept. Finally, four years after opening Casa, as all of St. Louis began to call it, he sold to General Mills but stayed in charge of operations for the restaurants bearing his name.

Casa Gallardos spread faster than spilled grape soda. The first branch was at Manchester and Interstate 270, then another at 270 and New Halls Ferry. Nashville was the first out-of-state site. By 1983, there were twenty-five of them. Three years later, General Mills sold the brand to W.R. Grace. Ray Gallardo, as he'd come to be known, tried to buy them back, but the larger bid from Grace won. Ray left the company. Things seemed to slip further and further away from what he'd envisioned.

Nevertheless, he persisted and, in 1989, opened the Casa Gallardo Grill at the then-brand-new Galleria, a second-floor restaurant with a mesmerizing rotating grill, tableside guacamole mixing and some serious, upscale food. Duck tacos, anyone? That eventually closed, but he's been involved in Ramon's Jalapeno, Patrick's, Bevo Mill, Ozzie Smith's and, with his wife, Ann, City Coffee House and Creperie.

The original Casa Gallardo is now occupied by Fuzzy's Taco Shop. So many things go full circle—but not nearly as many folks are having their first Mexican food experience at Fuzzy's as did at Casa Gallardo, we suspect.

Chuck-A-Burger

Chuck-A-Burger is the only restaurant in the St. Louis area that still has carhops. Just pull into any of the parking spots nosing up to the building on St. Charles Rock Road, and someone will head out to take your order. The only thing missing is the tray to hang from the car's window. "You kids would take 'em," mock-growls Ron Stille, the owner-manager, to yet another customer who comes in full of nostalgia. Then he and the customer laugh wildly. The alums of Ritenour High School, which is beyond the athletic field just across the street, are, of course, particularly fond of the place.

Chuck-A-Burger began in 1957; cue the sound of "A White Sport Coat (And a Pink Carnation)." Drive-in restaurants were the rage. Bud Taylor opened the first Chuck-A-Burger at Page and Pennsylvania. He owned IBC Root Beer (you can read more about him in the discussion of Carl's Drive-In). At first, it was a root-beer stand and then a frozen custard place. He brought Ralph Stille into the business about 1955, and the two decided to serve food. The next location was the Rock Road one. Another six followed, including 8411 Gravois, 9955 Highway 66 (Watson Road), North Florissant Road, two on North Lindbergh Road, one at Patterson, another at McDonnell Boulevard and one at 3150 Elm Point Industrial Drive in St. Charles. By 1965, there were ads offering franchises.

They were a magnet for teenagers, although that was hardly the only group scarfing down the hamburgers made with ground chuck—thus the name. Nevertheless, the socializing, particularly at night and on weekends, could be loud, if usually happy. The parking lots could get very crowded, and occasionally there were problems with loitering. At one point at the Gravois location, a quarter was charged for a token, which got a vehicle onto the parking lot. The token could be exchanged for twenty-five cents in food or drink.

In 1969, St. Louis had about two hundred drive-ins. It was the high-water mark for them before their nemeses, the-fast food restaurants, began to win the turf war. The very next year, the number of carhops began dwindling.

In time, all the locations except 9025 St. Charles Rock Road closed. Ralph Stille and his wife, Charlotte, eventually sold the business to his son Ron, he of the laugh line about trays. The menu is very similar to what it was in the heyday, including throwback favorites like pizza burgers and barbecue burgers with slaw. It's the same chili recipe as it's always been, and they have cherry Cokes. Oh, there's a salad or two, but back in the day, when a guy took a girl for a date, neither of them would have ordered a salad. The music is deliberately nostalgic, with doo-wop, rockabilly and the like.

Despite all that, burgers weren't quite enough on their own, and Ralph Stille began casting about for another way to encourage business. Vintage cars have proved to be the answer. The drive-in hosts get-togethers of fans of old cars several times a year and has become the meeting spot for several car clubs. (For a while, there were swap meets of old car parts and even baseball cards.) They've proved to be so popular that traffic has been, from time to time, a problem that the Stilles and the St. John city council have dealt with. But the events have become a fixture.

Chuck-A-Burger isn't one of those sanitized chrome wannabe places. It's the real thing, including fine flat-grilled burgers that will keep young relatives happy while their elders are identifying people in photos and songs being played. All that makes it a worthwhile stop.

The establishment has no active website, but it's on Facebook.

Chuck-A-Burger
9025 St. Charles Rock Road, St. John
314-427-9524
facebook.com/Chuckaburgerdrivein

Courtesy Diner

Where would American society be without the diner? While the midwestern diner tradition is different than that of New England and what once was called the Industrial East, they're still part of our heritage. At a certain point, it's just simpler to sit down at a counter, stare at a menu and order up a favorite breakfast or sandwich fixed just how you like it, right there in front of you. No putting up with that affront to human dignity, a pre-ketchuped hamburger kept warm under a light.

St. Louis still has the Courtesy Diner. More accurately, we have Courtesy Diners. Plural. We nearly lost them.

They began as Courtesy Sandwich Shops in the midst of the Great Depression, in 1935. At one point, there were at least a dozen of them, many in St. Louis, the others in small to midsize cities, with one glaring exception. It seems there was one in lower Manhattan, in a neighborhood of small businesses that were mostly what we'd now call electronic stores. Then it was just Radio Row, described nostalgically by one man as a place where his father and other men would go searching for just the right tube that would make the family radio work again. The diner was a lunch spot for employees and shoppers—although one story described it as "one of those uniquely New York luncheonettes," which it was not.

Then a big project came up, and the State of New York decided to take those properties by eminent domain. The little guys stood up on their hind legs and sued, in a case called *Courtesy Sandwich Shop, Inc., et al. v. Port of New York Authority et al.* The little guys lost, the courts holding that if the tax collector collects more taxes by taking the private property of one party and

Sign outside the Courtesy Diner on Hampton.

transferring it to another, that's a public use permitted by the Constitution. What? The name of the project? The World Trade Center.

At one time or another, there were Courtesy Sandwich Shops in St. Louis at 6800 Delmar, 2300 South Grand at Shenandoah, 3028 South Grand north of Arsenal, 3540 Gravois near South Grand, 7800 Ivory, 8701 South Broadway just north of River Des Peres and 1801 Olive. The latter location was transformed when the movie *White Palace*, from the novel by the late St. Louis author Glenn Savan, filmed some scenes there. It is the diner where Susan Sarandon's character works. (It's still operational and called the White Knight Diner.)

By 1997, there was just one left, at 3155 South Kingshighway, near Southwest High School. Leon and Helen Burrow bought it and changed the name to Courtesy Diner. Things went well, and a second location was built on Hampton near I-64 just two years later. In 2013, they added a third location, this one in St. Louis County, on South Laclede Station Road, just south of Watson.

Courtesy, as it's known locally, is not one of those Hollywood-type places that make a shiny high-end parody of the diner. It's an everyman type of place. The people-watching—and, dare we say it, the eavesdropping—is often great fun. A group of obvious regulars discuss world politics from their side of the coffee mug. Young mothers meet up, bringing babies in carriers. Faces often seen on television, whether as part of the news or in commercials,

A slinger, St. Louis's iconic hangover preventative, from the Courtesy Diner.

arrive in running shoes and baseball caps. Tattoos of all vintages are on display, especially late at night. So square it's hip? Patti Smith loves it when she's in town on tour.

Breakfast is available around the clock, and so is St. Louis's all-purpose meal, the slinger. A slinger? Potatoes—here, hash browns—are topped with a hamburger patty, chili and a couple of eggs. Cheese, onions and jalapeños are optional. The chili is from a company called Edmonds, a St. Louis tradition that's an offshoot of the now-gone O.T. Hodge Chili Parlor. Reminding one of the Ozarkian roots of South St. Louis, variations are available, like the Hoosier and the Hangover, subbing out white sausage gravy and chicken fried steak. (These are only available from 11:00 p.m. until 11:00 a.m.) One of the underappreciated dishes here is their hamburger, flat-grilled and arriving fast and hot.

Still twenty-four/seven, the place is still worthwhile.

Cash only; there are ATMs on-site.

Courtesy Diner
3155 South Kingshighway, St. Louis
314-776-9059

1121 Hampton Avenue, St. Louis
314-644-2600

8000 South Laclede Station Road, St. Louis County
314-553-9900
courtesydiner.com

The Crossing

Jim Fiala's first job in a restaurant was at the Village Bar. One should not call that venerable West County outpost a dive bar, but it's an extremely low-key place known for its red-and-white-striped exterior, shuffleboard and hangover-dark interior. The menu is, and always has been, bar food.

It's a much greater distance between the Village Bar and the Crossing, Fiala's restaurant in Clayton, than the ten or so miles on the map. Fiala is a local guy. He was going to have a career in finance. His job at the Village Bar was just while he looked for that position in finance. Then he realized that wearing a tie and sitting behind a desk sounded utterly awful. A few months later, a job as a deckhand on a cruise ship rotated him through the galley, and that led to the "aha!" moment. He loved the cooking, and he loved thinking about food, how it worked and how flavors combined—he was off! He went to culinary school and then began to work in some very serious restaurants, beginning with Spiaggia in Chicago. He then went on to Restaurant Daniel in New York, to work with Daniel Bolud. That's where he met Cary McDowell, who would eventually be his partner for several years in the Crossing. They both talk about peering out from the kitchen the night Tim and Nina Zagat, the founders of the Zagat guides, brought in their St. Louis editor, the restaurant critic of the *St. Louis Post-Dispatch*. The two chefs worked together at a resort in Puerto Rico and discovered that their ideas meshed well together. Eventually, they came to St. Louis and worked together for several years before parting ways.

Interior of the Crossing dining room.

The Crossing, named because the owners felt like it was crossing French and Italian styles of cooking and taste, opened in the spring of 1998. It was upscale, no doubt about it; at the time it opened, entrées were in the seventeen- to twenty-five-dollar range. And it was a hit. More important, it has stayed a hit, although, these days, a solo diner can walk in on a weeknight and have a bite in the bar without a reservation.

It was a tribute to the founders' credentials that when Thomas Keller of the French Laundry's first cookbook came out, the benefit signing was held at the Crossing. It's a tribute to the actual performance of the restaurant that Alain Gayot, scion of the French family that helped found the Gault-Millau guides and who oversaw their expansion into the American market, had dinner there a year later. (He then went off to Ted Drewes for a nightcap.)

It still perks right along. There was, for a while, a sibling called LiLuMa, an American bistro in the Central West End. Now another sibling, named Acero, in Maplewood, is Italian-ish. But the mothership carries on with a host of regular customers.

Almost as important is a cadre of regular employees. Their valet, Blake, has been with them more than twenty years. Regulars trust him so much that he was asked to valet a customer's car to Dallas. He did, of course. The service is smooth, knowledgeable and adept at sensing a table's mood. They know the menu extremely well, despite the frequent changes according to what's in season and what the kitchen has found that strikes its fancy.

The kitchen's executive chef is a man with quite a story of his own. Thu Rein Oo is in his third year of running the kitchen. He was hired as a dishwasher. Born in Myanmar, he spent two years in a refugee camp. In 2007, he came to the United States to live with his uncle in Indianapolis and then moved to St. Louis. A friend of his, also from Myanmar, who was working at the Crossing, suggested he apply for a job there as a dishwasher. As Fiala watched him work, after a while, he realized he'd found a gem. Thu took on more demanding roles, learned, watched and thought, all the while encouraged by Fiala and his associates at the restaurant. He says his favorite thing to cook is fish. And he's now an American citizen.

In the back of this book is a recipe for one of the Crossing's signature dishes, a warm cheese soufflé that arrives with crostini at every table to welcome guests. Fiala says that some people were puzzled by this when he opened. "Aren't you going to charge for it?" they would ask. The idea, he says, is to get people to relax and understand they're going to have a good time. Maybe they're craving pasta with black trumpet mushrooms or tenderloin with a Bordelaise sauce. Or they're not quite sure what they want but are ready to discuss options after they've had a little wine and a couple of crostini with the cheese mixture.

The Crossing will make you feel comfortable—and, it goes without saying, well fed. Even if you're not a regular.

The Crossing
7823 Forsyth Boulevard, Clayton
314-721-7375
thecrossing-stl.com

Culpepper's

Most people don't know that there was a Culpepper's before the mid-1970s.

Indeed, it goes all the way back to 1934, just after the end of Prohibition. A liquor store called Robinson Culpepper opened at 4908 Maryland, on what is now called Maryland Plaza. The store was among the customers buying from a distributor called Tony Faust's Sons, surely the offspring of St. Louis's legendary restaurateur whose fabulous establishment is discussed in *Lost Restaurants of St. Louis*. Business must have been good in those thirsty days. The following year, they moved across the street to what the newspapers described as "a spacious showroom" at the northeast corner of Maryland Avenue and North Euclid, which became their permanent home.

Before 1935 ended, the store's liquor ads also included the enticement "St Louis' Smartest Cocktail Bar," so it was clearly serving liquor by the drink. (That same year, the St. Louis excise commissioner ruled that women were not allowed to sit at bars. A newspaper story included indignant remarks from female patrons at various bars in town, including Culpepper's.) By 1939, Isadore Emas, at one time a bartender there, had purchased what had become Culpeppers Inc.

Things were still carrying on by the mid-1950s. An ad from the time proclaimed it to be Culpepper's Pizzeria and Cocktail Lounge, emphasizing the thin, crisp crust and seven kinds of pizza on offer. It was clearly one of the local hot spots. Bob Goddard, the gossip columnist for the now-defunct *St. Louis Globe-Democrat*, often discussed what he'd learned within the four walls. Some wit defined the place as "the poor man's Racquet Club," the squash-obsessed old-school private men's club a block or so away. (A middle-of-the-night fire in 1957 at the real Racquet Club was marked by a member living in one of the private rooms upstairs directing the firemen—axes, hoses and all—to use the service entrance in the rear. And the firemen complied.)

Things slowed way down, and it closed in 1975, then opening as a place named Ginger's, which was run by local restaurateur Lynn Smith. Smith would go on to give St. Louis places like City Cousin and Blanche's.

In 1977, the location returned to its original name after being bought by Herb Glazier and Mary McCabe. That iteration is the one that's legendary. McCabe ran the kitchen, and Glazier oversaw the rocking atmosphere. It was first and foremost a spot for adults, with a series of dictums beginning with a sign announcing that Culpepper's preferred not to serve children under twelve and evolving to a set of rules on the menu. There was, eventually, a reputation as a singles bar, but whoever heard of a singles bar that served lunch to people watching the passing parade at that busy corner? It came closer to a club. The place was so busy that at times it had, in effect, maître d's—one of whom, in fact, was Lynn Smith. Another was Jake McCarthy, the *Post-Dispatch* columnist who worked at bars while the paper was on strike, as it was in 1973 and 1978–79.

The menu was short, but the food was remarkably good, including a variety of excellent soups and, first and foremost, the chicken wings. It appears that Culpepper's was the first in town to serve what we now know to be Buffalo wings. The bar, of course, did a booming business, helmed for many years by the great Jack Rinaldi. Glazier did it all his way. He sold beer in cans because, he said, it got colder that way. He wouldn't stock swizzle sticks; they clogged up the vacuum cleaners. When patrons asked for them, he told them to use their spoons

Glazier and McCabe sold it in 1988 to several local buyers, one of whom was reported to have said that there would be no changes except that they would now serve decaffeinated coffee, ending another Glazier policy. But things did change

One bartender told the story of a woman who ordered a glass of wine. When he delivered it, along with her companion's drink, to her table, they were deep in conversation. Soon, though, the man came over to the bar. "You forgot the straw," he said.

"A straw?" asked the bartender, thinking he had misunderstood the order.

"The straw for the wine," explained the gent. The bartender handed him a straw.

Soon the man was back. "It's the wrong kind of straw. She wants a wine straw," he announced.

It turned out that she wanted one of those tiny hollow plastic swizzle sticks. Thank goodness this happened in the post-Glazier years; mollified, she drank her wine.

The new owners added other locations: Westgate Center in Creve Coeur, on Kirkwood Road and in St. Charles. The soups began arriving in giant plastic bags. High chairs appeared. The wings remained, though, but the crowd drifted off to other places. Now only a St. Charles location remains, and the original location is being consumed by the World Chess Hall of Fame. The corner's oldest remaining tenant is gone.

It was a strange, quirky, tasty place. As one local put it when hearing of the closing, "They treated all ninnies the same, no matter the race, creed or nationality. They were the purveyors of a special kind of snobbery and decorum I appreciated."

Cunetto's House of Pasta

Has Cunetto's House of Pasta been open only since 1972? It seems so ageless that it wouldn't be surprising to see hanging, unnoticed behind the bar, a picture of Pierre Laclede and Auguste Chouteau chowing down on plates of bucatini with Bolognese sauce. For most St. Louisans, it's pretty much been there forever. Vince and Joe Cunetto opened it. The Cunetto brothers were, of all things, pharmacists who'd had several drugstores both on the Hill and elsewhere. There was, explains the family, always food going in the back room for various lucky friends and customers. As the big pharmacy chains began eating up neighborhood drugstores, the brothers saw the writing on the wall. Reasonably priced pasta, they apparently figured, was their next adventure.

They took the building at Sublette and Marquette, very visible from Southwest Avenue, and gave birth to their House of Pasta.

It's a casual spot, no reservations except at lunch, and popular enough that waits are common. The waits are eased by a drink in the good-sized bar. The entertainment is seeing if any parties leave the premises without a bag of leftovers. This is classic St. Louis Italian, enough food to feed folks a second day, and servers are so accustomed to it that travelers who won't have access to a refrigerator in their accommodations usually receive a sympathetic apology. A fair number of out-of-towners are mixed in with family groups, since the word of mouth about Cunetto's has been around for literally generations.

Cunetto's House of Pasta.

It's not just pasta; the menu shows chicken, fish, a couple of steaks and of course veal. But the pasta goes beyond the expected ravioli/lasagna/meatball axis and into the unexpected, like several vegetarian options and quirky things like pasta di alba, with beef gravy, cream and Parmesan cheese. The kitchen shows proper respect for the underappreciated anchovy, with two kinds of pasta with different anchovy treatments.

Cunetto's is still in the family, run by Vince's son Frank and with a staff including some longtime employees. Frank sometimes talks about new items on the menu. He's referring to things that have been on the menu for only twenty or twenty-five years. That's tradition, St. Louis style.

Cunetto's House of Pasta
5453 Magnolia Avenue, St. Louis
314-781-1135
cunetto.com

Cusanelli's Restaurant

Most St. Louisans who knew Cusanelli's restaurant think about the suburb of Lemay. Indeed, it sits at the intersection of Lemay Ferry Road and Bayliss Avenue. But there were more restaurants by that name in the relatively recent past.

At that intersection, people may not know they're passing a historic building. Behind the white façade of Cusanelli's Restaurant is a building that may be close to two hundred years old. Some handmade bricks are still part of one wall. There certainly has been an inn on the site for that long. William F. Alden's book *It Happened in Lemay* says that the Marquis de Lafayette was feted on the site during his visit to St. Louis in 1825. He was honored with a dinner, at which he considerably overindulged and had to spend the night rather than return to St. Louis. Other guests over the early years included author Washington Irving, President William Howard Taft when he visited Jefferson Barracks and a cordwood peddler who left town owing a small bar bill. The peddler, Ulysses S. Grant, went on to lead the Union army and eventually the United States of America. Another notable and frequent guest was William Clark, the explorer and fourth governor of the state of Missouri. His home was at Bayless and Union Road.

We know for sure that this building was in existence by 1884, when Balthazar Risch founded Risch's Grove that year. Risch, and then his son and daughter-in-law, Alex and Margaret Risch, ran what came to be known as Risch's Eight Mile House. The name, says legend, refers to the distance—accurate to within an inch—from the Old Courthouse downtown at Broadway and Market to the building. For much of that time, there was an outdoor garden for dining, a good idea considering St. Louis summers. The Risch family operated it until 1949; after that, it continued as Eight Mile House until 1954.

That was when Nicola Cusanelli and then his son Dan took over the restaurant and named it after their family. The father and son, with mom Savina in the kitchen, began serving Italian specialties, including pizza, as well as traditional American food. They modernized things, adding a carryout window and carhops, at least for a while. Air conditioning came in 1955, something so important that they advertised its arrival. An artist created a large mural in the dining room. Around the time of the ten-year anniversary, the establishment was advertising special early-week dinners for two dollars, a bargain even then.

The restaurant hit a sweet spot between a family place and slightly upscale. People still rave about the fried chicken, and the steaks, which were surprisingly reasonably priced, were very popular. One early review remarked on the number of high chairs in the dining rooms. The lasagna was highly regarded, but there seems to be no record of whether the cheese on the thin-crust St. Louis–style pizza was the characteristic and sometimes controversial Provel. (You'll learn more about it in our section on Imo's Pizza.)

The very first Cusanelli's was at 4054 Chouteau at Sarah. Nicola opened it in the early 1930s and closed it around 1952. There's not much information on that one, but another Cusanelli's opened at 4015 West Pine in 1951. Like Rossino's a few blocks away, with which it is occasionally confused, it was in a basement, but this time it was the basement of the family home. Run by Dr. Paul Cusanelli, Nicola's brother and a graduate of St. Louis University Medical School, this Cusanelli's was primarily a pizzeria. Cozy and full of red-checked tablecloths, it drew the young, not just SLU students but residents of the many apartments in the neighborhood and, in time, of the legendary LaClede Town to the east. It also became something of a late-night hangout for the Playboy Club bunnies. His son, Paul Jr., eventually ran things, and sometimes one would see his other son, Joe, a professional singer who worked on Broadway and spent a great deal of time on the Muny stage. (Fanny, his daughter, also sang at the Muny, among other places.) By 1962, the name had been changed to Bandera's, but it was the same menu and personnel. That lasted until 1973, when Paul moved elsewhere and Joe-the-singer came home to reopen it under the original name. The building is gone, replaced by a parking garage, with no apparent record of when the restaurant closed.

Delmonico Diner

It is, in some ways, more than right that one of the city's best-known soul food restaurants was only a couple of blocks from the see-and-be-seen French-influenced Balaban's on North Euclid Avenue. The Delmonico Diner was the creation of Eva Bobo, who began cooking when she was eight years old, according to her family. She was assisted by her daughter, Dorothy Dunn. It was as casual as Balaban's was formal, with a short cafeteria line and ladies piling food on a diner's plate as it was passed from hand to hand. Macaroni and cheese and peach cobbler abounded. Pork chops, of course, and meatloaf were pretty much always there, as well as various kinds of greens, all cooked to velvety tenderness, tasting of smoky porkyness and one kind of pepper or another. Two different *Post-Dispatch* writers carried on at length about the quality of the lima beans, not usually a vegetable to excite the press.

Smart breakfast guests arrived before they sold out of biscuits, but everyone could take advantage of eggs perfectly cooked to order. The menu board referred to hash browns, but what waited on the steam table were fried potatoes with a good proportion of onion to raise the dish into perfection. The usual breakfast meats were on offer, but also things like Polish sausage, cut in quarters and grilled to crisp it up, and fish cakes.

It felt very neighborhoody—Bible study groups might meet in an alcove on the east side of the dining room while men with open newspapers discussed city hall or sports teams. The tables and chairs were in their second, or perhaps even third, rounds, sturdy but no longer fashionable and surely having had Sunday dinners in private homes spread across them in years past.

That made no difference to most folks. Muhammad Ali came to visit in 1987 and spent a good while at the restaurant, autographing books and kissing babies. By 1997, Rams wide receiver Isaac Bruce had become a regular patron. He might have had a hand in Delmonico's being hired to cater lunch one day a week at the team's training camp.

Mrs. Bobo died in 2005, but the restaurant carried on until it closed in 2011. Regulars glance at it as they pass and sigh a little.

Forum Cafeteria

The first memorable thing about the Forum Cafeteria, directly across Seventh Street from the entrance to Famous-Barr, was the art deco-ness of it. Even people who never heard of the style rhapsodized about the spun aluminum rails and chairs and the striking black-and-white tile. Most of us were surprised to discover that the establishment was part of a chain.

Clarence M. Hayman opened the first Forum Cafeteria in Kansas City in 1921. The name was a play on "for 'em"—for them, meaning everyone. The St. Louis site, which he opened in 1929, seems to have been the first time he ventured beyond Kansas City. Eventually, there were Forums in Cleveland, Chicago, Minneapolis, Los Angeles, Houston and Miami. Many of the locations were very handsome, the one in Minneapolis placed into a former movie theater.

Hayman was particularly clever in choosing the St. Louis location, in the very heart of shopping and offices and movie houses. It served three meals a day, and it wasn't just the Friday after Thanksgiving that lines of patiently waiting customers went out the door and down the block. It was very large, with two levels of seating. The mezzanine level was particularly popular, and scoring a seat overlooking the first floor was considered great good fortune. Employees carried trays for older guests and children who needed assistance, especially getting upstairs. It could be tricky to get to an open seat, especially in the winter, as coats draped over the backs of chairs. Tables were packed in, and sharing tables was common.

The former executive chef for the chain, St. Louisan Ollie Sommer, reported that during the post–World War II years when he worked there, they served an average of 1,500 to 1,900 breakfasts a day, opening at 6:00 a.m. to workers from places like Produce Row. During the war, when gasoline rationing was stringent and public transportation heavily patronized, Forum ads encouraged the public to leave home early, have a leisurely breakfast there while reading the paper and then proceed to work. (After the war, automobile traffic boomed downtown, and many local businesses, including the Forum, gave discounts at parking lots.) During the 1930s and '40s, its ads also made the point that eating there was actually cheaper than eating at home, without the work and the possibility of waste.

As with most cafeterias, it was hard to avoid the eyes-bigger-than-your-stomach syndrome. Everything was made from scratch. There was a butcher on the payroll, and things like the egg noodles in the chicken and dumplings were rolled and cut by hand. The tidy line before diners bewitched the eye. Salads started things off, pastels of coleslaw-type dishes followed by various jewel-colored gelatin choices, lacking only a sapphire blue to equal anything found up Locust Street at Mermod-Jaccard-King, the carriage trade establishment. Slices of pie and cake stretched in diagonal lines, but the most remarkable thing in the dessert section may have been strawberry shortcake. Somehow, even in the middle of winter, the strawberries were fresh, a remarkable thing in, say, 1954, and they were not priced as though they were caviar or lobster. The berries and glossy thickened juices had a faintly sweet biscuit as a base.

Main courses for many people often began and ended with something chicken. The Forum's chicken pot pie has been frequently and fondly remembered, and at one point, the kitchen would prepare 340 of them just to start the day's lunch. (The recipe appears in the back of this book.) But there was plenty of fried chicken, too, especially in a pre–Colonel Sanders world. Summers reported that he served 1,500 to 2,000 orders a day. The fish that St. Louis calls jack salmon is actually whiting, and it appeared daily at the Forum, not just during Lent. Young ones learned how to bone the fish easily, leaving them with lifelong skills with which they, in turn, would dazzle their own kids. Meatloaf was popular, as were stuffed peppers and salmon croquettes.

When Jamestown Mall opened in 1973, it included a Forum Cafeteria, which lasted until 1988. The year 1975 brought the debut of a Forum in Crestwood Mall. The malls were already drawing much business from downtown, and in 1977, the Forum on Seventh Street closed. By that time,

Harry H. Pope, of Pope's Cafeteria, who had become a major Forum stockholder, was quoted as saying that downtown cafeterias were suffering. The Jamestown location remained open until 1988; the closing of the Crestwood location cannot be determined.

One of the definitions of *forum* is a "public meeting place where ideas can be discussed." That's pretty reasonable in these circumstances, especially if the topic was chicken.

Gioia's Deli

It's a small yellow brick building at the northeast corner of Berra Park just south of I-44. (No, the park is not named for the former resident of the neighborhood, the Hill, Lawrence P. "Yogi" Berra, but after an alderman.) Constructed from material salvaged from the 1904 World's Fair, Gioia's Deli was for many years a grocery store run by Charlie Gioia. When he retired, his sons Steve and Johnny took over.

But in 1980, Cathy Donley's family bought it and turned it into an Italian delicatessen. One of the things that came with the purchase was the recipe for a sausage called salame di testa. In Italy, the salami, to use the American spelling, is made in different ways, depending on what part of the country you're shopping in. This version arrived in St. Louis with Charlie, who came from near Milano. It became the specialty of the house. The Donleys have exactly one copy of the recipe. It's kept in a safe.

Gioia's is known for its hot salami sandwich. "Hot" doesn't refer to peppery, but rather to the temperature of the sausage. It's thickly sliced to order; customers get their choice of bread, cheese, garnish and condiments. Metalmouths can go for pepper cheese, jalapeños or giardiniera salad and sriracha mayonnaise, but there are other condiments as well. Many people want theirs on the garlic cheese bread and continue building from there.

There are plenty of options for sandwiches at Gioia's, but it's the hot salami that has brought the place into the national spotlight. In 2017, it received a James Beard American Classics Award. One man came all the way from the United Kingdom to St. Louis to check out the sandwich.

The mural on the north wall of Gioia's Deli.

What the hordes find is a lunch crowd—Gioia's doesn't do dinner—that waits patiently in line. Some tables and chairs are inside and more are under an awning on the south side of the building. Probably the majority of sandwiches are carried off, to be eaten anywhere from Berra Park to someone's desk between phone calls. They're often accompanied by the house's tortellini salad or perhaps a bag of the St. Louis classic Red Hot Riplets potato chips, one of a particularly wide assortment of kinds of chips.

What, someone wonders, is so special about their salami? It's not like the salami you get at the grocery store or even practically any other sausage shop. The establishment makes more than 1,600 pounds a week of salame di testa. In Italy, it was originally made from hog parts like the head and trotters and tail, the whole thing braised, picked off and chopped up, then the thickened juices from the cooking used to moisten the mixture and all of it stuffed into natural casing before cooking again. Gioia's uses beef as well as pork, and they aren't using the leftovers from anyone's butchering. But the seasoning is just what it used to be, and the result is a very soft sausage with a gentle chew. As Marvin Hamlisch wrote in *A Chorus Line*, it's one singular sensation.

The Donley family is very serious about quality and service. They're patient with newcomers, who, despite the wait, haven't quite made up their mind about exactly what they want on their sandwiches. And about the quality? They very quickly pulled out of a location in Busch Stadium in 2018 because the operator to whom they'd rented their name and allowed to sell their salami wasn't doing it the way it should have been done.

There are two newer locations; in 2016, they opened downtown, and in 2018, in Creve Coeur, one of the western suburbs. The salami is still made across from Berra Park. And, says Alex Donley, the next generation to run Gioia's, yes, Yogi himself would come in—hot salami with mustard was his standard order—whenever he was back in his hometown.

Gioia's Deli
1934 Macklind Avenue, St. Louis
314-776-9410

903 Pine Street, St. Louis
314-776-9410

623 North New Ballas Road, Creve Coeur
314-776-9410
gioiasdeli.com

Charlie Gitto's on The Hill

Charlie Gitto's on The Hill is one of the insider secrets in St. Louis's Italian neighborhood. Okay, it's been open since 1981, so maybe it isn't so much a secret, but it seems to fly beneath the radar, clicking along and satisfying diners.

People do get Gitto *padre e figlio* mixed up. Charlie Sr., who passed away in the summer of 2020, ran Charlie Gitto's Downtown, which began when he franchised a location of The Pasta House Co. That spot, close to Busch Stadium, is more casual and has a different menu. Charlie Gitto's on The Hill, owned by Charlie Jr., is the location where Angelo's was for many years.

As is the case with so many Italian restaurants, there's a story to that, as well. Angelo's may or may not have been the place where toasted ravioli was invented; you can bet the house that we're staying out of *that* argument, at least for now. Relevant to our story, though, is that Charlie Sr. worked there as maître d', and soon, young Charlie, age eight, was, too, doing things like wrapping baked potatoes and cleaning up behind the bar.

Fast-forward to 1981. Charlie Jr.'s father was ensconced downtown, feeding shoppers, businesspeople, sports fans and people whose business was sports, especially baseball. Charlie Jr. was working in Dallas at a black-tie restaurant when he heard that Angelo's was for sale. He took a deep breath, headed home, borrowed some money and bought the place.

As with many young businesses, it was a struggle at first. The first January they were open, 1982, brought the paralyzing snowstorm that officially dropped almost fourteen inches on us. They did no business at all for two

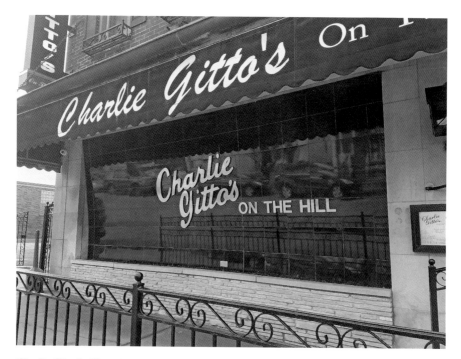

Charlie Gitto's, Shaw Avenue on The Hill.

weeks. But in nice weather, the patio on the west side of the building charmed. David Slay, who was then the hot young restaurateur in town, enthused over it, especially when enjoyed with oysters and some of Gitto's pasta.

Interior designer Robert Lococo re-did the decor in 1989. The interior, quiet and tasteful, is headlined, for some, by the bar. It feels like something out of Hollywood's glamour days—shining dark wood, curved and deeply padded booths and white tablecloths. It's seen its share of bold-faced names, a lot of athletes and plenty of entertainers, many of them sent by concierges at the best hotels. Vincent Price, the native St. Louisan and esteemed gourmet—no fumbling cook himself, either—came whenever he was back in town. Merv Griffin sulked after an unexpected run-in with a television crew. But the most memorable visitor may have been among the least noticed.

Joe DiMaggio came for dinner. He arrived with—well, no one was quite sure if it was what we'd now call an entourage or just security people. DiMaggio, who was shy when he was young, became extremely reserved as he got older. After he retired, he limited the access that media and indeed most of the world had to him. He slipped into the restaurant surrounded by his people, was taken immediately to the back dining room, which was

The old-school glam of the barroom at Charlie Gitto's on The Hill.

empty, and ate. "Nobody even saw him except his waiter," says Charlie, "and me—I got to meet him." His departure was, similarly, dramatically silent. But it was DiMaggio, the legend.

It's a good choice for groups of diners that include both the traditional and more adventurous, with the daily specials often things that one might not expect in an Italian restaurant, like lamb with a mango sauce, for instance. A recipe for their penne Borghese is in the back of this book. Service generally hangs at the sweet spot between chilly and hovering. They've also started a commissary and are making their own bread, pizza dough, desserts and other items.

Yes, there is still toasted ravioli on the menu, and they make their own, not the frozen mass-produced stuff. They've been feted for it nationally several times, including a 2001 Food Network series that spent a week on The Hill. It was Gitto's that fed the program host a lunch of toasted ravs.

They've opened another Charlie Gitto's at Hollywood Casino in Maryland Heights with a similar but not identical menu. A third location in Chesterfield suffered storm damage, and its reopening is still in question. But, as is often the case in such things, the motherhouse is still rocking it.

Charlie Gitto's on The Hill
5226 Shaw Avenue, St. Louis
314-772-8898
charliegittos.com

Goody Goody Diner

St. Louisans who happened to be watching the A&E show *Live Rescue* on the night of April 23, 2019, discovered very near the end of the show the St. Louis Fire Department responding to a call for a restaurant fire. It took a few minutes for the cameras to reveal the distinctive white-and-red exterior of Goody Goody Diner. The show ran out of time at that point. Out-of-towners had no idea what was in flames.

Opened in 1948 in a former A&W Root Beer stand, over the years, Goody Goody had gone from being just another small eatery to a stalwart of the neighborhood and, indeed, of the city of St. Louis. Richard Connolly's parents, Herb and Viola, bought it in 1954. They quickly put the thirteen-year-old Richard to work.

It was a busy restaurant in a busy neighborhood. Four automobile dealerships were nearby. The General Motors plant farther east on Natural Bridge ran three shifts a day. Goody Goody served breakfast, lunch and dinner every day of the week. It seated thirty-eight, many at the counter, but it also had carhops, one of the many jobs Richard Connolly was pressed into service for. ("That was the best," he recalls. "I got tips. You don't get tips peeling potatoes.")

The front expansion to the sidewalk came in 1957, and more room was added in 1968. That was the year Richard took over the business. But the neighborhood was becoming quieter. Carhop service ended in 1972. The GM plant was slowing down, the dealerships were moving. By 1977, "Dinner didn't make any sense," says Richard. It became breakfast

Diner mugs at Goody Goody Diner.

and lunch only. And then, in what proved to be a brilliant move, it made breakfast available all day.

Breakfasteers cheered. Business picked up. In 1998, Judy Evans, the food editor of the *St. Louis Post-Dispatch*, brought Jane and Michael Stern, the authors of *Roadfood* and other similar tomes, in for a bite. Goody Goody was not only in their next book, it was also in their column in *Gourmet* magazine in 1999. It became a place where Black and White diners easily mixed, not something St. Louis does enough of. In that sense, it's reminiscent of the late, legendarily multicultural LaClede Town development. For years, the diner was a place where cops would go to eat. Then a different sort of civil servant became noticeable. Elected officials were having meetings there with constituents and other politicians. One day in May 2000, with only a few minutes' notice, Vice President Al Gore, who was making a presidential run, came in to press the flesh for a while and then grab a little food to go. Claire McCaskill dropped by during a campaign. And in 2016, Joe Biden appeared to chat with diners about voting for Jason Kander. Cedric the Entertainer? Miss America? For sure.

The breakfast menu was broad but traditional. Fourteen different meat options went with the eggs, including salmon cakes and Polish sausage. How do you want those eggs? The menu explained in detail eleven ways of cooking and the relative texture of them. The difference between scrambled medium and scrambled hard? Right there for all to see. Toast, biscuit, English muffin, bagel or three silver pancakes, your choice. Potatoes, grits or rice? And that wasn't even getting into the omelets, including the signature Wilbur, filled with hash browns, onions, peppers and tomato and topped with chili and cheese. Goody Goody was also an early adopter of the chicken-and-waffles movement.

Employees, as mixed as the customers, often stayed a long time. Many days, customers were met by Sly Bell, de facto maître d' and plateside poet in the style of Muhammad Ali. He came on board in 2010. The dining room had been expanded even more in 1990 to seat 110, and a takeout counter kept busy.

To the surprise of many, Richard Connolly and his wife, Laura, sold the restaurant in 2014. He'd been approached before, he said. But the time was right to retire. The new owners were brothers Ryan and Joe Safi and their brother-in-law Charlie Mustafa. They owned convenience stores nearby. And they intended to keep things pretty much as they had been, except that they would open on Sunday, which hadn't happened since dinner was cut from the schedule. Breakfast all day, but still no dinner.

Then came the fire. The blaze started in electrical equipment in the kitchen, said the St. Louis Fire Department, and the kitchen, said the *Post-Dispatch*, was destroyed. The restaurant was boarded up.

More than a year later, the building was demolished. Attempts to reach the owners have produced nothing. Many, many people mourn its loss.

Goody Goody Diner
5900 Natural Bridge Avenue, St. Louis
goodygoodydiner.com

Hendel's Restaurant

I f you never felt that St. Louis was a gaggle of small towns that eventually morphed into a city, visit Hendel's Restaurant in Florissant. On a quiet corner in a neighborhood that feels like a village, it looks as though it's been there for decades. The building certainly has. Hendel's Restaurant and Market is somewhat newer.

The building dates to 1873. Fifteen or so miles to the southeast that same year, James Eads was completing work on the first road-and-rail bridge across the Mississippi River. (The bridge opened the following year, after an elephant was led across it to prove that it was safe.) Meanwhile, in Florissant, 599 St. Denis Street (note the French spelling) became a general store and grocery.

We don't know who owned it at first. But in 1915, the Hendel family bought the property. They kept selling the groceries and added a butcher shop. It was a mainstay of the town, which became a suburb of St. Louis, and stayed in the family until Henry and Marge Hendel retired in 1993.

After 120 years of selling groceries, the building was bought by Ed Bennett and remodeled into a restaurant. Bennett's primary job was as the coordinator of the small business and management program for St. Louis Community College. As part of his job, he taught a class called "How to Start a Restaurant." Bennett put his money as well as a fair amount of sweat equity where his mouth was, doing some of the remodeling himself. He kept the previous family's name and opened Hendel's Restaurant in 1994.

The two-story brick building with an outdoor dining area behind it has a cozy feeling, matching the architecture and the neighborhood. The menu works hard to find the sweet spot between safe and interesting, and it accomplishes that. A conservative eater can find a hamburger or pasta with meatballs; the adventurous can try short-rib tacos or grilled scallops. The crowd tilts the same way. Folks have found a home.

There was a great deal of happy kerfuffle in 2014 when the pastry chef at Hendel's, Lia Weber, and Al Watson, with whom she used to work at the bakery Wedding Wonderland, entered TLC's *Next Great Baker*. The St. Louisans won the first week—and kept on winning. They ended up in the finals in Las Vegas against a couple of guys from New Jersey. Lia and Al won the whole thing, including the chance to manage Buddy "Cake Boss" Valastro's Las Vegas bakery and a nice wad of cash. In a twist of the *Godfather* line, they took the money and left the cannoli to come back to St. Louis and stay here. Lia, whose sister Christina and brother-in-law Nathan Bennett run Hendel's, is now opening her own bakery in Florissant. But Tuesday nights were pretty exciting at Hendel's during the competitions.

It's a place that just keeps keeping on. About the biggest news is that they don't serve Sunday brunch anymore, just lunch. The regulars were disappointed, but they still come, just as North County folks have been stopping on St. Denis Street for more than a century.

Hendel's
599 St. Denis Street, Florissant
314-837-2304
hendelsrestaurant.com

Imo's Pizza

Okay, so it's a chain. It wasn't in 1964, though, when a couple of St. Louisans began a delivery-only pizza place on Thurman Avenue near the Missouri Botanical Garden. No one was delivering pizza in those days; you went in, sat down and waited for it to be baked.

My, how Imo's has grown. Now there are more than one hundred Imo's Pizza locations. The style it helped create marks "St. Louis style" pizza that's popping up in other cities as a sort of novelty.

According to Ed and Margie Imo, those aforesaid St. Louisans, the idea took root when, every Friday night at 11:30 p.m., they would order a pizza. Good Catholics who didn't eat meat on Friday, they'd figured out that by the time it was a little after midnight, the restaurant would have their meat-topped pizza ready. But wouldn't it be nice if it could be delivered? It took a while to save up the money, but in a few years, they were ready, with a used pizza oven, a couple of refrigerators and a seventy-five-dollar stove. He worked, she worked and her brother did the deliveries.

In less than a year, friends asked if they could open a second store for them. By 1980, there were fifteen stores; by 1985, there were thirty. It wasn't until about that time that the percentage of pizzas that were eaten off-premises, whether carryout or delivered, reached a significant number in the St. Louis market. (That includes Imo's and other stores.)

It's hard to generalize about one hundred stores, all but a few of which are franchises, but most of the ones around St. Louis, which is where the mass of their business is by far, are focused on pizza to go. Some have dining areas, all very simple; some have beer and wine; and some have pickup windows.

The Imo's Pizza sign at Hampton and I-64, perhaps trying to lure animals from the zoo across the highway.

But what about the pizza? The first element in this, and all St. Louis–style pizza, is an incredibly thin crust. Even the Imo's website describes it as "cracker-crust." American appreciation of pizza crust as a specialty of its own is a fairly recent thing, long after the 1964 birth of Imo's. There is no rim on the crust, thus the paucity of ranch dressing at an Imo's store. (It's available for your salad, though.) A tomato sauce with a hit of oregano and toppings go all the way to the edge.

The add-ons list contains nothing unusual. But the cheese—that's a very different story if a customer isn't from these parts. Or even perhaps if their parents aren't—we know of several cases in which kids raised hundreds of miles away plead for Imo's when they return to town to visit the grandparents. Perhaps it affects the DNA.

Provel cheese is on an Imo's Pizza. What is Provel cheese? It's a processed combination of Swiss, cheddar and smoked provolone cheeses, soft and with a low melting point. Unlike mozzarella, it doesn't stretch out when a piece of pizza is lifted from the whole pie or a bite is taken. It's tidy. The smokiness is pretty subtle until it's tasted solo, but it surely adds to the overall flavor of the pie. Imo's has finally begun to sell Provel in grocery stores, both shredded and sliced, since it's become popular on salads, too. (It also makes a fine grilled cheese sandwich, report young cooks.) Where and how it began is sufficiently convoluted that its history was the subject of a research paper at Washington University in St. Louis. According to the late Joe Bonwich, restaurant critic and food writer at the *St. Louis Post-Dispatch*, an anthropology major was exploring how specific foods become intertwined with local communities' identities. The student also discovered that it was being sold in 1955 in Dayton, Ohio. (Obviously, they didn't appreciate it as much as St. Louis does.) The well-known chef and restaurateur Lidia Bastianich discovered Provel when she came to St. Louis for a book on Italian food in America and included a recipe for St. Louis–style pizza. She talks about its complexity and umami.

Imo's pizzas are always cut in squares. It's only been in recent years, when pizza has become more studied in popular culture, that St. Louisans have realized that this is occasionally called tavern cut or party cut. The usual line is that Ed Imo was a tile worker when the first store opened, and he was so used to cutting things at right angles that the pizzas were cut that way, too. It's another reason, like the Provel cheese, that these are very tidy pizzas—and St. Louis does like tidy.

In 2015, a new headquarters was created downtown a block from City Museum with a restaurant and a shop for Imo's branded items, including frozen pizzas and that five-pound block of Provel you need to take back to Dayton with you.

Detractors have come up with some fairly amusing descriptions of St. Louis–style pizza, at least the first hundred or so times they're heard. But when it comes to Imo's, it's obviously a serious success.

Imo's Pizza
Multiple locations
imospizza.com

Kemoll's

Joe and Dora Kemoll, who'd been married only about a year, opened a small store at North Grand and Penrose in 1927. It was a mark of the times that these weren't the names on their baptismal certificates. Joe was born Vincent Camuglia. After he came to the United States from Sicily, a desk sergeant in the army decided it would be an easier name for him to spell. Dora was Gaetana Danna.

The store was a simple little place, serving sandwiches and ice cream to the neighborhood, which had a fair mixture of business and homes. They were three blocks north of Fairgrounds Park, which was three blocks north of Sportsman's Park, what St. Louisans now might refer to as *old* old Busch Stadium. The Cardinals and the Browns both played baseball at Sportsman's Park, and for a while St. Louis University's football team used it as home field. Obviously, there was plenty of activity in the area. Dora did all the food herself and even then was known as being meticulous in what she sold to customers. At first, they lived behind the store, but things went well, and the restaurant expanded. The family moved to an apartment upstairs.

By 1934, the year after Prohibition ended, they had a liquor license, and a very active bowling team as well. In 1942, the family purchased the entire building, which had six apartments upstairs. After the war, things continued to prosper. An ad from 1949 noted that they served "pizza" (in quotation marks), spaghetti, meatballs and Italian ravioli. By 1953, another ad was explaining that they served pizza every day.

Food was clearly becoming more of a focus for the family as they aimed higher and higher gastronomically. In 1954, Mrs. Kemoll had a recipe in

Kemoll's original location, in a photograph at its newest spot in Westport Plaza.

the *St. Louis Globe-Democrat* and later that year did a cooking demonstration for cannelloni, described as Italian meat tubes. They had, she said, tasted a delicious version at a restaurant in Milan when they were visiting the previous year, a prophetic remark. That same year, an ad asked, "Have you ever had a tuna fish steak?" In another couple of years, ads talked about braciole, a rolled, stuffed beefsteak and linguine with fresh clams—indeed, clams were often found on the menu.

The year 1961 found the Kemolls expanding to four hundred seats. Daughter Mary Rose married Frank Cusumano, who'd come on board to help manage. The football Cardinals, the Big Red, had arrived down the street in 1960, making for even more traffic, although, of course, the Browns had decamped in 1953. Nevertheless, the stadium was on its last legs, and a new one was finally opened downtown in 1966.

It was not a coincidence that Kemoll's began its Gourmet Nights that same year. "People," explained Mark Cusumano, grandson of Joe and Dora and son of Frank and Mary Rose, and now the manager, "didn't have to travel to Grand and Penrose to find an *ordinary* restaurant." It should be worth the customer's trip, and they set out to achieve that. Gourmet Nights were themed multicourse meals. At first, each was devoted to a different part of Italy, with the food of that area, all carefully researched and reproduced by the family and the kitchen staff, although eventually, they expanded to cover other areas as well. Nine courses were $6.75 in 1968; wine and a tip were not included.

It may or may not have been coincidence that the Big Red management, and some of the players, too, were extremely fond of Kemoll's. The restaurant has always been friendly to pro athletes. Charley Winner, the coach who arrived the year of the move, was an avid fan of the restaurant, especially Gourmet Nights. The public-relations person for the team, no wimpy eater himself, reported that Winner, for a relatively little guy, could put away a lot of food. Winner brought along, among others, the team photographer, Herb Weitman, the selfsame PR guy and their spouses. There's a certain irony that the PR guy's next gig was as the restaurant critic for the *St. Louis Post-Dispatch*, a job he held for twenty-three years.

After much thought, the family decided in 1989 to move the business downtown to the Metropolitan Square Building. The first-floor quarters, dark and quiet, not unlike some restaurants in northern Italy, had marble floors and several small dining rooms off a long corridor, making things seem more intimate than a restaurant that actually seated three hundred. They took the top floor for catering in 2003 and, in 2009, moved the restaurant to the fortieth floor. That wasn't quite at eye level with the Arch, but it surely felt like it. The previous dining rooms had felt cozy, but this was an elegant ballroom-sized chamber.

Leases run out and tastes change. The newest iteration of Kemoll's adds the phrase "Chop House" to its location in Westport Plaza, just off I-270 and Page Boulevard. There is a little less of the Italian food, a little more of the meat and fish that people have gone for in this era of paleo diets. A Kemoll's chicken dish of Sicilian heritage is in the back of this book. The fried artichoke hearts are on the menu when they can get the right fresh ones, and so are the cannelloni Dora Kemoll was explaining to St. Louis so many years ago. It's some old, some new. Kemoll's is evolving, just like it always has.

Kemoll's Chop House
323 Westport Plaza, Maryland Heights
314-421-0555
kemolls.com

Mai Lee

In 1978, the Tran family of Can Tho, Vietnam, was in trouble, and things were only going to get worse. Three years earlier, what we in the United States knew as the Vietnam War had ended. But the government of the now-united Vietnam was still watching for people they thought had been involved with the losing side. Sau Van Tran kept being called to the police station in their hometown, and he kept lying to them about what he'd done during the war. If they found out the truth, he'd be imprisoned—or worse.

He took his family's savings in gold and booked passage for his wife, Lee Vo Tran, and their infant son on a vastly overcrowded boat of 107 people to escape to Thailand. The boat was attacked by pirates, but eventually, they made their way to a refugee camp. Mr. Tran thought he remembered his army ID number. The Americans helping process the refugee camp eventually tracked down his history, and the family qualified as refugees.

Sponsored by the First Unitarian Church, they were brought to St. Louis. None of them spoke English. He got a job as an auto mechanic. "Mechanics are mechanics," said his boss, Dave Monnig, later. "It's a language of its own. You give a guy a headlight and he knows where it goes."

Wise words, Dave Monnig. It's true of food, too. It's a language of its own. Lee Tran began working in small Chinese restaurants, watching how it was done. In 1985, they opened Mai Lee in a tiny storefront at I-170 and Delmar. They served Chinese food, but after a little while, she started to offer a few Vietnamese dishes as weekend specials. It was so popular that

The greeting at Mai Lee.

they began serving Vietnamese food every day the restaurant was open. Lee ran the restaurant; Sau kept his outside job, coming in to help on weekends.

In the winter of 1986–87, the *Post-Dispatch* restaurant critic got wind of the place. He knew nothing of Vietnamese food, he acknowledged. And there were language barriers. But, he acknowledged, "In my typical style, I just blundered ahead." He was very happy with what he found. Mai Lee became the first of many Vietnamese restaurants in town.

They expanded three times at that location, going from six tables to twenty. Brightly lit, sparkling clean, with embroidered tablecloths under glass tabletops, it drew people of all persuasions.

In 2010, the restaurant moved. The location was something of a challenge. No one recognized the name of the street, Musick Drive, and the restaurant wasn't visible from nearby Eager and Hanley Roads. But there was a Metrolink stop very near, and—important to St. Louisans—a huge amount of parking, much of it covered. In addition, there was a forward-thinking, next-generation Tran who was now strongly involved in running the restaurant. Qui Tran, the baby on the boat, has picked up the pho (the famous Vietnamese soup) and run with it, so to speak. He was the one who advocated for this spot.

The place thrived. They doubled their floor space. The lovely decor is a collaboration with Qui's sister Sara Tran, who does interior design. Old customers returned, and a whole new group has appeared. The bar is busy with some drinkers and a fair number of solo diners. Service is fast and efficient. And, always a heartening sign in a restaurant, there's a certain amount of chatter between tables—"What's that you're having? It looks good" and "Be sure and have the Vietnamese coffee!"

Qui has opened another restaurant, Nudo House, which specializes in ramen, and there's already a second location for it. Nudo House's pho was featured on the cover of *Food & Wine Magazine* in February 2018. But Mai Lee represents the family roots, where they settled in, worked hard and flourished.

And the Vietnamese coffee really is good.

Mai Lee
8396 Musick Drive, Brentwood
314-645-2835
maileestl.com

Mammer Jammer

Sometimes, tiny, word-of-mouth restaurants can mark the personality of a city. Richard Anderson's little place, Mammer Jammer, was one of those. Originally—at least as far as research can take us—it was at the wedged corner of Lindell and Olive, now a politely mowed grassy lot. It opened around 1978. Most of the business was takeout, as there were a lot of offices nearby—the major movie studios had offices within a block or so, and there were still some doctors' offices in the old University Club Building. It was open late, too, which meant it helped to absorb a certain amount of alcohol before partying folk drove home or brought cops or newspaper folks after a shift.

The focus of Mammer Jammer was a sandwich of the same name. Oh, there were other things: chili and burgers and some barbecue, even tripe sandwiches. But it was the MJ that drew folks the first time and in all subsequent visits. A soft, hero-sandwich-type roll was split and spread with what had to have been Cheez Whiz or its generic equivalent. It waited while the beef, sliced as though it were going in a cheesesteak, sizzled on the grill. Peppers—both jalapeños and red flakes—and onions were thrown on top, and "clang!" things began. A rapid chopping and tossing, with a fine rhythm, the cook, usually Anderson, working with a spatula in each hand. When it was all done just right, the meat and vegetables were piled on the bun, waiting on a sheet of aluminum foil, and the whole was topped with some brown gravy.

The entrance to Mammer Jammer. *Courtesy of Robin Winfield.*

How much heat could the diner tolerate? Eight degrees of heat—or lack thereof—ran, per the carryout menu, like this:

Regular—No fire. For the faint hearted.
Mild—First hint. Just a little tingle.
Hot—Spicy. Taste the peppers.
Extra Hot—You like living on the edge.
Super Hot—You've got one foot over the edge!
Mary Francis—The hottest highsteppin' mama in town!
Big John—Rest in peace! Notify next of kin!
It—You are in The Here After.

The sign went on to say, quite unnecessarily, "We Offer the Hottest Sandwich in Town."

The sandwich was rolled in the aluminum foil, but between the heat and the moisture, only the most agile diner would try eating one standing up without a large towel tucked into their collar. It quickly became knife-and-fork food, but no one seemed to complain. Of course, the It did get ordered; one man recalls that his son while in his early teens boasted that he could handle it. The young man couldn't speak for the remainder of the day.

For a while at that location, the sign read "Mammer Jammer Stockade," but the final word disappeared in 1998. St. Louis University bought the building and tore it down, so Richard Anderson and his sandwiches moved three blocks east to 3131 Olive, where they settled in to the back of Mr. Andre's Lounge, an establishment that provided alcoholic refreshment. Then there was a spot on North Kingshighway, but it finally landed at 5124 Natural Bridge, with two tables and five or six chairs. Sandwiches continued to be produced until it closed in 2012.

Nothing has ever quite taken its place.

O'Connell's Pub

W hat becomes a legend most?"
That was the slogan that Blackglama Mink used decades ago, showing off pictures of famous, glamorous women—and a few men, like Rudolf Nureyev and Luciano Pavarotti—sporting glossy fur coats. But the phrase stuck around for a long time, and it's a fitting one to use for O'Connell's Pub.

More than sixty years ago, a neighborhood emerged at the corner of Olive Street and Boyle Avenue in the city's West End. It began with antique stores. Then a nightclub appeared, then bars and more music and clubs, as well as some restaurants. It came to be called Gaslight Square, and it gave locals a chance to hear new performers, see improvisational theater, have dinner and drift from bar to bar to catch up on gossip or favorite musicians. The area had a national reputation as being hip, even avant-garde.

Part of that group was a saloon that called itself O'Connell's Irish Pub. Ray Gottfried; Jack Seltzer, who was a real estate guy; and Frank Mormino, who went on to own the Europa 390, opened it in late 1962. Mormino soon sold his interest to Dick Draper. Draper owned an antiques shop, told tall tales and once claimed to have owned the only hippopotamus farm in Missouri. The pub drew well. It was cozy and dark and served London broil and unusually large hamburgers. The poet Allen Ginsberg, of *Howl* fame, drank there, sitting by the fireplace and carefully removing his shoes. He was far from the only notable client. No live music, with the exception of bagpipers who came by every week or so. There was plenty of talk, though, with a fair number of local writers and other literary types and theater people.

But Gaslight Square was a nova, a star that flared and then returned to its earlier, quiet state. As things slowed, the owners wanted to sell, and in 1965, the pub's bartender, Jack Parker, bought them out. Places closed, and the crowds left. But O'Connell's, and Jack Parker, stayed.

For a number of years, the establishment must have made enough money to stay afloat, But, in August 1972, Parker moved O'Connell's to the corner of Kingshighway and Shaw, to an ancient saloon originally owned by Anheuser-Busch. There were still regular customers at the old location in the decaying neighborhood, but not enough. Would they make the two-plus-miles trek to the new location? Were the Missouri Botanical Garden and The Hill good neighbors for such an establishment?

It had been a difficult decision for Parker. One of his longtime customers had just signed on as the restaurant critic at the *St. Louis Post-Dispatch*. He implied in print that it was "the dumbest move ever," as he later explained to his wife (me). He and Parker laughed about it for years.

The "new" location, now more than four decades old, feels like it's been there forever. Much of the artwork came from the old place, including some

O'Connell's Pub.

still-misidentified pictures. It's dark, to the point of inducing near-blindness when entering at the height of a summer day, but the eye adjusts to the warmth of old wood and the glow of brass chandeliers, survivors of a building at the 1904 World's Fair. It feels so right that an Anheuser-Busch commercial was filmed at the bar. A long table bisects the dining room, a throne-like chair at its head.

When things are busy, as they are most weekends, for instance, there's actually a velvet rope to corral the patiently waiting diners. The ghosts of the original incarnation must look down in head-spinning astonishment at that rope, the only vaguely pretentious thing in the place. It's always nice to see multigenerational groups, with young people being initiated into the traditional pleasure so far beyond fast food. Nevertheless, it's definitely an adult-oriented spot.

The excellent hamburgers remain, nine ounces big. Diners who forgo a bun find that the dish is steak-like in its beefiness. Roast-beef sandwiches costar to great acclaim. The remainder of the menu is relatively short—various good soups and a weekly rotation of daily specials, like Thursday's roast pork sandwich. Food does not arrive quickly, since the burgers are cooked to order. O'Connell's has always been a place for conversation, and it's fun to see people relax, put down their phones and just talk to each other.

Service is knowledgeable but brisk, occasionally brusque. Many of the employees stay decades, in the kitchen, on the floor and behind the bar—people like Norah McDermott, a native of Tanzania, who didn't suffer fools lightly; and the late bartender Red Garner, who told stories about people like Zsa Zsa Gabor and Tommy Smothers. Bartender Lenard Voelker has retired but returns every week or so to trade stories. Jack, who died in June of 2020, was often upstairs, running a small antiques shop, discussing his racehorses and chatting up the occasional visitor. These days, Jack Parker's nephew Fred, usually bartending, and his son John are in charge of things.

"Time is precious," says an entry on O'Connell's Facebook page. "Slow down and enjoy it." O'Connell's seems like a good place to do that.

O'Connell's Pub
4652 Shaw, St. Louis
314-773-6600
saucemagazine.com/oconnells

The Piccadilly at Manhattan

How can you resist a restaurant famous for its chicken pie and servers outfitted in T-shirts sporting a silhouette of a hen with the Greek letter *pi* inside?

It's safe to say that chicken pot pie on the menu means a place that's either cutting-edge hip or very traditional. The Piccadilly at Manhattan is definitely the latter. Opened in 1901, which means it was serving people while the Louisiana Purchase Exposition was in the planning stages, it appears to have been a tavern at first. Then, in the 1920s, Niccolo Colloida opened the Piccadilly Buffet. Was it a buffet by our modern use of it? A number of small tavern/restaurants that were still around in the sixties in St. Louis used the word, along with phrases like "merchants' lunch," but didn't offer what we'd call a buffet. All-you-can-eat or not, it stayed in business.

Niccolo was soon joined by his son Paul. At Paul's passing, Tony and Phyliss Colloida came into the business with Niccolo. They updated things like windows and siding in the mid-1950s. Nick and Maggie Colloida did a big restoration in 2007, but it still feels like a neighborhood restaurant, both in architecture and clientele. Not that outsiders get the cold shoulder, but the welcome to everyone is warm. Their daughter Molly Cooper is now running things. There's a patio in the back, much of it covered, feeling a great deal like a back porch. The bar works as a place to wait for a table or just to have a meal. That chicken pot pie has a sibling made with short ribs and a little mashed potato, for instance, and plenty of fried chicken from grandmother's recipe fly by on plates. Smoked rib-eye steak can be

The Piccadilly at Manhattan.

an entrée or part of a sandwich. Many speak highly of the hamburgers. Individual fruit cobblers are the dessert of choice, always blackberry and another, quarterly, choice.

Reservations help, especially for guests who are going on to functions at Webster University like the Repertory Theatre or Opera Theatre of St. Louis. But folks who have some flexibility can play it by ear. And there's always the possibility of a late, leisurely lunch while playing hooky.

The address is in the name, Manhattan Avenue being the intersecting street. And if you have trouble finding it, the website has directions.

The Piccadilly at Manhattan
7201 Piccadilly Avenue, St. Louis
314-646-0016
thepiccadilly.com

Pope's Cafeterias

Pope's, St. Louis's largest home-grown cafeteria chain, got its start in industrial food. Harry A. Pope worked for International Shoe Company in 1915. It had been formed four years earlier with the merger of the Peters Shoe Company and the Roberts, Johnson and Rand Shoe company, and it would become the largest shoe manufacturer in the world. (Does anyone remember the old line about St. Louis: "First in shoes, first in booze, last in the American League"? The last referred to the St. Louis Browns baseball team.) Two of those names are tied to a building at Barnes-Jewish Hospital known as Rand Johnson.

Harry was big on efficiency and felt that the people who worked for him needed hot lunches. He came up with an idea for preparing large quantities of food and developed carefully measured recipes to make sure of a consistent result. In ten years, Harry went from being a foreman to the head of personnel at the company and overseeing kitchen operations that produced fifteen thousand meals a day.

In 1933, his sons Harry H. and Edwin opened Pope's Cafeteria at 3538 Washington in what is now Grand Center. Even in those days, the neighborhood was a buzzing center of entertainment with several large movie houses. The building, which today houses Jazz at the Bistro, had been everything from apartments above ground-floor businesses and organizations, including the Spanish consulate, to a hotel and, lastly, one of five YWCA cafeterias. The boys put their father's ideas to work. Despite the continuing Depression, business went well, and three years later, they took

The first Pope's Cafeteria location near the Fox Theatre in Midtown, now Grand Center. *Courtesy of Missouri History Museum.*

over an existing business, an outlet of Child's Cafeteria, at 808 Washington downtown. Harry Sr. resigned from International Shoe and plunged into things. Pope's also opened or ran industrial cafeterias in other businesses, beginning in World War II, but its public face was the tray line at its two retail locations.

The original location near Grand was used in a movie filmed in St. Louis in 1953. *The Great St. Louis Bank Robbery* is about the robbery of Southwest Bank at South Kingshighway and Southwest Avenue. It stars a young Steve McQueen. It was the first feature film for Charles Guggenheim, who would go on to win two Academy Awards. Guggenheim had been brought to St. Louis by the Ford Foundation to help open KETC, the public television station, and often hung out in the Central West End at Europa 390, a site discussed in *Lost Restaurants of St. Louis.*

Pope's was ahead of the curve with its move into suburban shopping centers. In 1956, it signed a lease for space in Northland Shopping Center. In 1958, it took space in an office building in Clayton and, the following

Vitrolite sign from the exterior of Pope's second location downtown on Washington Avenue. *Courtesy of Larry Giles and the National Building Center.*

year, came to Westroads, the predecessor to the St. Louis Galleria. Eventually, Pope's had locations in South County Center, West County Center and Northwest Plaza and in the smaller shopping plaza at Page and Woodson. There were other restaurants that didn't bear the Pope's name, like the Round Table and Seven Kitchens. Pope's even bought a part-interest in its rival, Forum Cafeterias, and eventually had a finger in locations in California and Switzerland.

Perhaps the signature dish of the group, aside from the salmon croquettes with creamed peas, was the nut torte. The recipe for that is in the back of this book.

Cafeterias have all but disappeared from the United States, with customers carrying their food away from restaurant kitchens in bags rather than trays and choosing by the availability of parking rather than the taste of what they're eating, at least according to some. Pope's, like so many family-owned businesses, even on as large a scale as they ended up, dwindled away as they were eaten by corporations.

Protzel's Delicatessen

In a town that respects "We've always done it this way," Protzel's Delicatessen surely hits the mark. On October 1, 1954, Bob and Evelyn Protzel, neither of them yet thirty years old, opened for business. It was a Friday, the first day after the High Holy Days. The location in a neighborhood in Clayton had originally been a small grocery store, the kind that was all over St. Louis in those days. They chopped and pickled, stirred and mixed, making most of what they sold. That included curing the meats and grinding horseradish, a job as tear-inducing as chopping onions.

Bob was apparently quite a character. He was ahead of his time in having two vastly different occupations simultaneously. Besides running the delicatessen with Evelyn, he was a wordsmith, both serious and silly. He wrote ad copy for companies like Anheuser-Busch, Adams Dairy and Community Federal Savings and Loan. And he wrote comedy, selling jokes to people like George Burns, Phyllis Diller and Henny Youngman.

That's how it worked back then. Writers sent in jokes, and if a comedian used them, they sent the writer a check. (Even Woody Allen started out that way.) Local-woman-made-good Diller used this one of Bob's: "You want my recipe for vanilla wafers? Put Clearasil on chocolate chip cookies." Youngman kept declining Bob's offerings but encouraged him. Finally, one night on *The Ed Sullivan Show*, Bob heard Youngman deliver one of Bob's jokes—without paying for it. He wrote an irate letter and got a check for five dollars, which, Youngman said, was his standard payment. Bob shot back, "I always heard Jack Benny was the cheapest guy in the business, but you've got him beat, you SOB."

Protzel's Delicatessen.

He and his pal Al, who owned a laundry on the block, played checkers and poker and had long talks solving the problems of the world. They were serious practical jokers. Once, Bob left a herring on a dryer in the laundry, where the odor was apparent, but the fish wasn't, for quite a while. (Al's revenge was a crab under the seat of Bob's car.) One business owner on the block consistently violated an unwritten rule: Leave parking places on the street for customers. Park anywhere else, but let customers have the street parking. One hot day, the miscreant blithely parked his convertible and opened his business. Bob and Al climbed to the roof of the delicatessen, armed. Together they lobbed a couple of dozen eggs into the top-down car. Thereafter, reports Bob's son Alan, the guy parked off the street.

The signature dish here is still the corned beef, and there's a story about that, too. One day a couple of years after it opened, a regular customer walked into the store. Mr. Braverman was a retired deli guy himself. He opined that the corned beef was good, but there was a particular secret that would make it better. He would tell Bob, with two conditions. One was that the recipe remain a secret. The other was that when Bob retired he pass it on to a young deli guy. He didn't ask for money, just a handshake. They're using the same recipe to this day.

Bob died too young, but with his apron on. Evelyn kept things up to her standards, which were uncompromising, helped by her sons Ron and Alan, who eventually took over. A wide variety of uncommon packaged foods, crackers, candy and condiments, were also offered. Ron, it was said, could discuss at length anything he sold, including the most esoteric. He knew the manufacturer, a couple of anecdotes and a suggested use. Baked goods in the front counter were from Pratzel's Bakery—the similar names always confused newcomers—including the upside-down cupcakes, especially the dark chocolate glazed ones with a tender and remarkably moist interior.

Now the corned beef recipe, and the store, is indeed in the hands of a young deli guy. Max Protzel and his sister Erica are the third generation running what the sign out front still calls "Bob and Evelyn Protzel's Delicatessen." Max and Erica still have dad Alan checking in frequently, but things are clearly in the groove.

It's not exactly what it was in the beginning, of course. The freezer case has lots of stockpiled delicacies, and there's considerably less of what the grocery world calls "fancy foods"—exotic mustards and so on. There is no more penny candy, but some uncommon candy bars are offered, and there is a wider line of soft drinks and unusual chips than ever before. Alas, Pratzel's Bakery has closed, so no more upside-down cupcakes. But there are tables and stools to eat lunch in the store and tables out front to enjoy Wydown's flowering trees, the Fernando Botero statue of the fat guy on the pony and the passing parade along with a Reuben sandwich.

Yes, a Reuben, with both corned beef and pastrami—and the traditional cheese. Protzel's is a kosher *style* deli, not a kosher one. You can take home some lox for breakfast tomorrow.

Protzel's Delicatessen
7608 Wydown Boulevard, Clayton
314-721-4445
protzelsdeli.com

Rizzo's Top of the Tower

The day the Gateway Arch was topped off, October 28, 1965, was the day that Rizzo's Top of the Tower opened. This was not just any rooftop restaurant. In particular, it pre-dated by three years the Top of the Riverfront, which crowned the Stouffer's Riverfront Inn.

Both of them are gone, and many people get the two confused, but it wasn't the Top of the Tower that revolved, it was their salad bowl. The Top of the Riverfront did revolve, leading to many merry stories about women placing their handbags by their windowside chair as they enjoyed the view, only to discover it gone when they reached for it—there was a nonrevolving inches-wide part of the floor on the outside wall. Returning from the restroom also caused confusion.

Neither of these drawbacks were present at Joe and Gus Rizzo's establishment, where the tablecloths were just as snowy white and the menu just as elaborate. Ten floors above street level as it faced Lewis and Clark Boulevard, it was one of the most upscale restaurants in North County. In the same complex, on a lower level that faced west, were a movie theater and a bowling alley. Retail space and business offices were on hand, both in the tower and in the building that abutted the tower to the north. Originally, there was to be a second tower, but that never panned out. The condominiums in the tower sold well.

The views from the restaurant were excellent. There in the distance was the Arch and downtown, and sunsets were wonderful. Weather-watching proved to be unexpectedly popular as thunderheads gathered. Private function rooms

An advertisement for Joe Rizzo's Top of the Tower. *Courtesy of Donald Casalone.*

were available, and lots of events like wedding receptions were held there. On weekends, various musical groups played and couples danced.

Mamma Anna Rizzo's tomato meat sauce was used on pastas, but there were plenty of non-Italian options, too, in the elegant room. A critic raved about the shrimp de jonghe. The signature dish, however, wasn't an entrée. It was the spinning salad, mixed tableside. It included an assortment of greens, a creamy dressing with some blue cheese, herbs, a pinch of Lawry's Seasoned Salt and chopped boiled egg. The spinning was done very gently once things were mixing so as not to bruise the lettuces. The garnish was an anchovy fillet. We have what is said to be very close to the original recipe in our recipe section in the back of this book.

It closed in the winter of 1991–'92, after the death of Joe and the conviction of an employee who had embezzled what was estimated to be more than $100,000. The building, now derelict, still stands, a weary ghost of the happy past.

Schlafly Tap Room

Once upon a time, boys and girls, there was only one brewery in St. Louis. (Before that, there were heaps of them, but that's another story.) The palazzo on Pestalozzi Street was unchallenged for decades until attorney and former English lit teacher Tom Schlafly got a wild idea. He wanted to open a microbrewery in the shadow of The King of Beers.

Dan Kopman was another local guy. He spent his junior year abroad at Edinburgh University and discovered the world of beer there. After he graduated from Kenyon College, he went to work for Young's, an English brewery, after interning there and at Scottish Brewers. He became an export manager in the United States and learned about microbreweries. Dan's father, Charles Kopman, a former law partner of Tom Schlafly, suggested the two get together. But knowledge was not the only thing Dan brought to the equation, as will be revealed.

Schlafly and Kopman opened the Schlafly Tap Room on December 26, 1991, in the old Swift Printing Building at Twenty-First and Locust Streets. They managed to get the first microbrewery license in the state of Missouri, which allowed them to brew 2,500 barrels a year, to be sold solely at their brewery. How did that go? In 2017, Schlafly brewed 45,000 barrels.

The neighborhood then was pretty abandoned. The streetlights didn't work, and the building itself was so derelict that it was set on fire for the apocalyptic *Escape from New York*, which was filmed here. Now, it's a

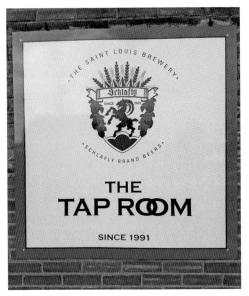

Outside the Schlafly Tap Room, a sign
done in the tradition of English pubs.

wonderfully roomy place—dining rooms, bars, a meeting room upstairs—all
deeply casual, of course. In the ensuing decades, the neighborhood has begun
to thrive, including the huge police headquarters only a block away and the
Major League Soccer stadium being built a few blocks south.

Originally, it was going to be in the English style, a pub at a brewery with
nothing more than potato chips—or crisps, as the British refer to them—and
similar packaged snacks. But Americans, they realized, weren't familiar with
that, so they used Susan Manlin Katzman to help develop a menu. Tom
Flood was hired as the restaurant manager and gave good input as well after
his years at Balaban's.

St. Louisans learned about real fish and chips, although the menu referred
to the latter as French fries, avoiding the confusion of the British-Irish name
for them. The fish was lightly battered, and the dish was served with the
options of a creamy herb sauce that wasn't quite tartar or a housemade
ketchup that charmed even the ketchup-avoidant. Hamburgers came on
English muffins, the better to avoid that bun-falling-apart-because-the-
burger's-so-juicy syndrome. The excellent G&W smoked liverwurst made
an appearance fairly soon, on rye bread, naturally, with onion slices. Beer
cheese soup. White chili that sizzled. It was food that tasted as good as it
sounded on the menu.

The crowning dish on the menu was and is the sticky toffee pudding. This
is another Kopman gift, specifically, the recipe of Sheena Kopman, Dan's

Scottish wife. Sheena had worked at the Udne Arms, a pub in Aberdeenshire, where it's said that one of the first versions ever of the dish appeared. It's a pudding in the British sense; we'd use the word *dessert*. What arrives is a large square of cake, dark and moist and swimming in a toffee sauce. Both of them are warm, and the sauce is particularly good late at night when it has thickened from being kept warm throughout the day. The lashings of whipped cream are a necessity to cut the richness. It's one of St. Louis's greatest desserts, and there's a recipe for it in this book.

Technically, a tap room is a room in an actual brewery. Schlafly was among the first in the country to open on that basis, and for a long time its food sales helped finance the brewing. That's no longer the case, but the focus for the company is still on beer. Schlafly involves itself in the community in a wide variety of ways. When the Pope visited St. Louis in 1999, it made a beer called Holy Smoke Papal Porter. Beginning in 2016, the four hundredth anniversary of Shakespeare's death, the brewery began making a seasonal beer for St. Louis Shakespeare Festival's June production in Forest Park.

Their second location, in Maplewood, at 7260 Southwest Avenue, opened in 2003 in a revamped grocery store. It produces the bulk of the company's brewed products. It, too, serves food, from a menu somewhat different than the original location's, but the sticky toffee pudding is served there, as well. The Maplewood location hosts a weekly farmers market on Wednesdays throughout much of the year. In addition, it's the home of the Schlafly Gardenworks, growing food for the restaurants, using sustainable practices in the one-seventh of an acre. It's drawn attention from people like author and television personality P. Allen Smith. At both locations, private rooms are often used for nonprofit meetings, part of their continuing community engagement.

Now that the folks on Pestalozzi Street are run by an international conglomerate, Schlafly is the biggest locally owned brewer in the state. But even if someone surpasses them—fat chance—they still won't have the finest sticky toffee pudding.

Schlafly Tap Room
2100 Locust Street, St. Louis
314-241-BEER (2337)
schlafly.com

Schneithorst's

One of the iconic restaurants St. Louis recently lost was Schneithorst's. Many people only remember it as being the rooftop bar and what was called the Kaffe Haus underneath at Clayton and Lindbergh, although the dining room and bar did some business as well. It was originally known as the Hofamberg Inn. But there was more to Schneithorst's than many of us knew about.

The Schneithorst family fed St. Louisans for more than one hundred years. Arthur Schneithorst Sr. began working at the legendary Planter's House but left to go to and eventually run Benish's Restaurants, a group here in St. Louis. The Depression did Benish's in, but Arthur persevered and opened the Rock Grill, a seafood restaurant. It must have done well; by 1937, he had also taken on the Bevo Mill's operation. (There's more on Bevo Mill in *Lost Restaurants of St. Louis*.) The family, including Arthur Jr., moved to the apartment behind the immense blades of the mill. They made sure the Bevo, as it was casually known, had an immense lobster tank like Benish's. Arthur Sr. passed away in 1947, but his son, who'd grown up in the business and gone to law school, kept things going—indeed, going quite well. Among the accomplishments after the end of World War II was Bertha Schneithorst, the matriarch of the family, entertaining the syndicated food columnist Clementine Paddleford. Paddleford said, "St. Louis folks eat what they like, and pay no mind to what's cooking in other cities." She relayed two recipes: one for gigantic cheese-stuffed olives that were said to be a favorite of the Busch family, the landlords of the restaurant; and the other for herring salad, which Mrs. Schneithorst claimed to be the best in St. Louis.

Arthur, like his father, was the entrepreneurial type. He took over the restaurant at St. Louis's Lambert Field in 1939 and advertised it as what we'd now call destination dining—a promise of "gobs of shoestring potatoes" with the fried chicken, and "succulent decapod crustaceans," as another ad referred to the lobsters on offer. It was described as being open twenty-three hours, fifty-nine minutes a day. In 1940, he began to operate mobile lunch counters at the Curtiss-Wright airplane plant across the runway from the terminal. (That plant closed after the war, but McDonnell Aircraft bought the facility.) He began making box lunches for the airlines, and by 1949, his catering company was described as the second-largest airline caterer in the world, with a total of seven hundred meals a day. By the mid-1950s, he was also operating restaurants in seven motels, mostly Holiday Inns, around the area. The airport restaurant was turned over to other people in 1955.

All of that was prelude to what was going to happen at the Clayton-Lindbergh site in Frontenac. In 1956, the Schneithorst family took a long-term lease on the southeast corner and announced plans to build a restaurant seating 460 persons and a drive-in section with phones at each stall where customers could order from the kitchen. It was christened the Hofamberg Inn and became the scene for banquets and wedding receptions in the rooms on the second floor.

The drive-in was an instant hit with teenagers and quite a contrast with the staid interior's crowd of adults. One former habitué of the drive-in reminisced about driving down to the Parkmoor on Kirkwood Road at Manchester to "confront the Kirkwood kids" before heading back to their turf. There was already another drive-in location, known as the Big Bevo, at 2210 Hampton, now the site of a QuikTrip. It wasn't just teenagers availing themselves of the burgers—often double patties with cheese and one version or another of secret sauce. It finally closed in 1979, probably a victim of the drive-through concept. The same year, the family handed off management of Bevo Mill to others.

German food in restaurants wasn't new to St. Louis, of course, and the family had been serving it at Bevo Mill. Here was a menu with stalwart Eisenhower-era mainstream food peppered with options like sauerbraten and schnitzel. It worked well, and the private rooms were popular for things like company functions and receptions. The décor in the large dining areas was meant to evoke a Bavarian beer hall, and servers in costume added to the atmosphere.

Food stayed pretty close to the middle of the road except for the German items, even as eaters across St. Louis became more adventurous. The establishment was raising its own beef on its farm in Clarksville by 1962. James Schneithorst Sr., the son of the younger Arthur, said in 1995, "We don't do trends." But bison burgers appeared on the menu alongside the braunschweiger sandwiches and Big Bevo burgers, bidding for the low-fat crowd.

The dinner crowds drifted away, and there were fewer private events. In 2002, the decision was made to tear down part of the building and put in retail and offices. They kept what would be the Kaffee Haus, the small bar and dining room and installed a beer garden on the roof.

In recent times, Schneithorst's was known for business breakfasts, leading to much table-hopping under the guise of networking. The menu still called appetizers *vorspiesen*, even though the first item was toasted ravioli. And the sausage was from G&W in south St. Louis, fine bratwurst and knockwurst. It was the longtime morning hangout of Jerry Berger—he always insisted he wasn't a gossip columnist, he was "a people columnist"— where he shmoozed and picked up tidbits. It wasn't hard to see recognizable faces there—Stan Musial often lunched at Schneithorst's after he retired. The pastel faux-rustic coffee shop that held the daytime traffic was a far cry from the dark, wood-beamed dining rooms of days gone by. The crowd had gotten older over the years, at least at ground-floor level, but the bar on the roof still drew a younger crowd, especially when the weather was right.

Financially, though, it apparently didn't make sense to continue. "Schneity's" became another place for St. Louis to remember and tell stories about. And we do like doing that. But where will we get G&W sausage with our eggs over easy?

Sidney Street Cafe

Way back when, St. Louis was rife with small corner retail shops, many of them groceries. By the middle of the twentieth century, there were still some around. We called them confectioneries, even though they weren't candy stores per se, or delicatessens, even though they seldom if ever sold sandwiches. One such location was at Sidney and Salena Streets, not far from the brewery. (For nonlocals, that's how we refer to the mother ship of Anheuser-Busch, now technically AB InBev.) More than 130 years ago, a red brick building went up for commercial use. As was common, it held apartments on the second floor. From 1925 to 1970, it was a bakery.

Three restaurants followed, the third being the Other Mother, a casual place run by Chuck Conners. It was his second, a companion to Mother's Pizza. Conners worked with kids who'd dropped out of school and successfully employed them at both places.

When it closed, a group of investors decided they wanted somewhere they could take their business clients for lunch and dinner. It opened on February 23, 1985. The quiet opening they'd expected for the Sidney Street Cafe didn't happen; it served six hundred customers before closing that night. It seemed a success, but even by the following year, it was losing money. It was sold to Tom and Lisa McKinley with her brother Greg Pohlman.

Things began to gather steam. The interior, brick walls, some plants, old photographs and antique sideboards showed that this was not a deadly formal place. Long tapers at each table were lit as guests were seated. The menu was presented on a tablet-sized chalkboard, and the waiter described in careful and often lengthy detail each dish. Both the appetizers and the entrées had become more elaborate. An ad for kitchen help warned that it was "a challenging menu." For a while, desserts were made by the gifted Tim Brennan, now owner of Cravings; one review described a chocolate cake as one that would make Betty Crocker wish she had become an Avon lady.

The Sidney Street Cafe was being seen as a special-occasion restaurant. The fact that dress was relatively casual surely didn't hurt. It was highly ranked in local restaurant polls and topped out in the Zagat guide ratings for St. Louis, which are also consumer driven. But not long after the Zagat was published, a bomb was dropped. The restaurant had been sold.

Kevin Nashan, who had cooked at Space and then Harvest (and more and bigger names before that, like Commander's Palace, Le Francais and Daniel), and his wife, Mina, a St. Louisan, along with his brother Chris, bought the Sidney Street Cafe in 2003. Regulars panicked, thinking their beloved had left them for some fast-talker from Santa Fe. One local publication even reassured them, writing, "The more things change, the more they stay the same."

That didn't prove to be the case, but the vast majority of those folks are now delighted about the results. Nashan adjusted things relatively carefully, but the menu evolved into something different, something exciting, with new ingredients and new combinations. Some of the old standards remain, like the veal dumplings appetizer and the lobster-stuffed filet with béarnaise sauce. Smoked duck? Confit of octopus? New choices. In 2004, a year after the change, one restaurant section noted that it was still a tough reservation even on weeknights.

Someone besides the locals was paying attention, it turned out. Nashan was a five-time semifinalist in the James Beard Awards for Best Midwestern Chef. He was a finalist in the category in 2014 and 2016. Then, 2017 saw him take the title as Best Midwestern Chef. He's opened Peacemaker Lobster & Crab just down the street and a second location of that in Tulsa. But the Sidney Street is still the bull's-eye for visitors and locals alike.

It is not, of course, an inexpensive restaurant. But if you want a little more of an idea why and how a restaurant like this operates, take a look in the back at the recipe from Kevin Nashan for the caramelized onion tart. It shows the complicated things kitchens like this do.

Still the candles. Still the chalkboard slates. Still feeding people very well.

Sidney Street Cafe
2000 Sidney Street, St. Louis
314-771-5777
sidneystreetcafestl.com

Sweetie Pie's Upper Crust

The most remarkable thing about Sweetie Pie's Upper Crust isn't that it had its own television series. (It's the only St. Louis restaurant with that distinction.) The whole story is pretty amazing, and to top things off, Robbie Montgomery's food is a delight.

Montgomery, born in Mississippi, came to St. Louis with her family when she was six. As a teenager, she sang at church and in a group from her building in the Pruitt-Igoe complex. They appeared in talent shows around town and were hired as backup singers. Their first recording was "A Fool in Love" as backup for Tina Turner. The original plan was to use another vocalist, but he didn't show up, and Tina sang her first recorded lead. It turned out to be a big hit.

Montgomery toured with Ike and Tina as one of the Ikettes, doing one-night stands. During this time, she developed a reputation within the group as being able to work wonders with a hot plate and a few pans. She went on to sing backup for other people like Barbra Streisand, Joe Cocker and Stevie Wonder. There was a gig at Carnegie Hall with Dr. John, a memorable night marked by the non-appearance of the singers' costumes. In a move worthy of Scarlett O'Hara, they used curtains, belts and glitter to fashion their own.

A lung problem put an end to Robbie's touring and most of her singing. She became a dialysis technician at what was then Jewish Hospital. One of her patients was Leon Strauss, the urban developer responsible for the renaissance of Grand Center. They spent five hours together three times a week and got to know each other. Strauss was a go-getter, dialysis or no, and

Robbie Montgomery, looking elegant and cooking up a storm.

he recognized the same quality in Robbie, who wanted to open a restaurant. Her determination meant that she did things like buying furniture for the proposed eatery piece by piece as she got the money.

Sweetie Pie's opened on West Florissant in Dellwood in 1997. It was a small place, doing lots of takeout from the short cafeteria line, but local musicians showed up with some frequency. A regular customer and fan brought in his photographs of her and an album cover from her post-Ike days as one of the Marlettes, managed by Tina Turner's sister, for décor in an expansion of the restaurant.

Closer to the center of the metropolitan area, she found a location in 2006 and opened Sweetie Pie's at the Mangrove, at the corner of Manchester and Tower Grove Avenues. The sunny corner even had room for a piano, and there was occasional entertainment. For a (too-) brief time, brunch was offered. The location brought more traffic, even before the Grove neighborhood became a beehive of gastronomic and entertainment activity.

The Grove location, though, still wasn't quite what Robbie Montgomery had dreamed of. She wanted a larger location, where she could have function rooms and places for group dinners, class reunions and wedding rehearsals. She'd had her eye on a spot at the northern edge of Grand Center. Leon Strauss, who died in 1999, and his wife, Mary, who had overseen the restoration and reopening of the Fox Theatre, worked with the landlord there to make sure it could happen. Sweetie Pie's Upper Crust opened in Grand Center in 2006, a half block from Powell Hall, the home of the St. Louis Symphony Orchestra.

The dining room at Sweetie Pie's Upper Crust.

The Upper Crust has plenty of room, a good thing, because tour buses still come through depositing loads of hungry folks ready to see if the elegant Miss Robbie—yes, elegant even in her chef's whites—really can make those pots and pans sing. *Welcome to Sweetie Pie's*, a reality show, premiered on the OWN Network in 2011 and ran for one hundred episodes.

The meatloaf and baked chicken are still there, and so are the greens and candied yams. Some of the best fried chicken in town (wings only, these days) and, in a nod to St. Louis, baked pork steak with gravy stand out, along with daily specials ranging from liver and onions to jack salmon, the local name for whiting. There is cornbread, of course, and not the kind that escaped from a cake-mix box, as well as the uber-cheesy macaroni and cheese she's known for and whose recipe is at the back of this book.

Several years ago, a cookbook came out with Miss Robbie's recipes and some stories. It was so popular that it was even sold as far away as Singapore. "Sweetie Pie" is Robbie's nickname, as warm as she is, although it is not nearly descriptive enough for a woman as strong and persistent as she obviously has been.

Sweetie Pie's Upper Crust
3643 Delmar Boulevard, St. Louis
314-932-5364
sweetiepieskitchen.com/sweetie-pies-upper-crust

Ted Drewes Frozen Custard

N o, Ted Drewes Frozen Custard technically isn't a restaurant. There are no servers, just busy young adults zooming around inside two white be-canopied buildings in south St. Louis. No tables or chairs, unless you count hoods or trunks of cars in the parking lots. People lean on vehicles, spooning up frozen happiness from green-and-yellow paper cups. But visiting this mecca of frozen custard—no, it's definitely not ice cream—is surely a St. Louis eating tradition.

On the first vaguely warm and sunny weekend of spring, both locations are mobbed—the Chippewa location is open most of the year. As the school year ends, traffic picks up, from families celebrating to teenagers stopping by as part of an evening out. On Thanksgiving weekend, short of a blizzard—a word we'll get back to shortly—it's filled with people home for the holidays and showing the next generation their old haunt.

Who was Ted Drewes? Ted Drewes Sr. was a fine tennis player, a Missouri champion who was looking for something to do in the off-season. In 1929, he tried selling frozen custard in Florida, but the following year he opened an operation in St. Louis, on Natural Bridge, next to another nostalgic favorite, Sam the Watermelon Man. The next year, 1931, the South Grand location just below Meramec Street opened. In 1941, the Chippewa store opened on historic Route 66. The Natural Bridge operation moved farther west a couple of times, ending up where the Normandy Post Office now is, before closing in 1958. The south side locations have never moved.

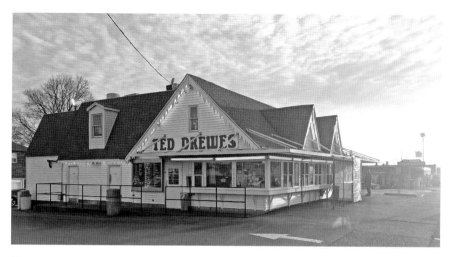

No crowd at the moment at Ted Drewes.

Frozen custard is not, by legal definition, ice cream. It has egg in it, and Drewes's recipe includes some honey, which amps up the flavor. And Drewes does something else that ice cream makers don't. Actually, it's the opposite: They *don't* do something the ice cream people do. Ice cream makers add what the frozen dairy industry calls overrun; they whip air into it. The federal government has a limit to how much air can be beaten into ice cream before it can no longer be called ice cream. Ted Drewes does no overrun, which is why that Cardinal Sin with tart cherries and hot fudge you just picked up is heavy. Flavors? To use the old line about the Model T, any flavor you want as long as it's vanilla, at least at the stores. At the two home bases, the flavors come from the add-ins. (Ted Jr. says the only flavor he regrets is the bunnycrete, with carrots, cream cheese, cinnamon and pecans. The attempt to catch the flavor of carrot cake just didn't work.)

The signature dish is the concrete. It dates to 1958, when a kid named Steve Gamber stopped by on his bike and asked Ted for the thickest milkshake he'd ever made. Ted, always customer-service savvy, complied. It was so thick that he handed it to young Steve upside down. A tradition was born. Now, concretes are always handed to customers that way. The variations are immense; rookies are advised to study the online menu to start to sort things out.

And that brings us to the aforementioned blizzard, although this time it will be spelled with a capital *B*. The Dairy Queen Blizzard came into existence because a big St. Louis franchisee, Sam Temperato, appreciated

So thick they're delivered upside down at Ted Drewes.

the concrete and began to think, "Hmmm…." He introduced the concept to senior officials at Dairy Queen, and the rest is history, as it spread throughout the company, increasing revenues almost everywhere. But we in St. Louis had the original.

Ted Drewes Jr., who took over as his father got older, and Travis Dillon, Ted Jr.'s son-in-law, still run things. There have been plenty of suggestions about franchising, but the family feels it's better to concentrate on what they do best, which is summed up in signs inside each of the stores. "Our Business Is Service," they remind each employee. They have, however, quite literally branched out in one direction: In 1953, Ted Jr. decided that, in the winter, they would sell Christmas trees. When the stores were closed for the season, the unused real estate of their parking lots, he thought, could be put to good use. They have a farm in Nova Scotia where the trees are grown. For a while, cups the size of the smallest concrete were filled with actual concrete and were sold alongside the trees as stocking-stuffer gift certificates. Nowadays, the Chippewa store stays open through the holidays, and people can, and do, eat real frozen custard while they pick out a tree. Truly choice trees on the lot are designated "Dottie trees," in honor of Ted Jr.'s wife.

The people-watching is always good. People of ages, wearing everything from swimsuits to business suits, and the occasional celebrity can be seen, as well as lots of tourists. A certain Frenchman, scion of a family whose name appears on one of those elegant restaurant guide series, demanded to be taken there. When he was Speaker of the U.S. House of Representatives, Richard Gephardt, whose district covered both locations, would bring back Ted Drewes (locals never bother to add "frozen custard" to the name) to his colleagues in Washington packed in dry ice. It was a highly coveted gift. But dry ice is available to anyone who asks, not just VIPs.

Today, Ted Drewes can be found in freezer cases at local groceries like Schnucks, Dierbergs and Shop 'n Save, and at a few movie theaters. There are several flavors available. And for those coming or going—or perhaps incoming visitors who can't wait a moment longer—St. Louis Lambert International Airport has installed three vending machines of Ted Drewes.

It's an authentic St. Louis Thing.

Ted Drewes
6726 Chippewa, St. Louis
314-481-2652

4224 South Grand, St. Louis
314-352-7376
teddrewes.com

The Tenderloin Room

"T he Chase is the place," was the slogan.
And the Chase Park Plaza Hotel certainly was "the place" for generations of St. Louisans who wanted proximity, or at least potential proximity, to the great and the glamorous. For many years, the very heart—indeed, the nesting place—of those big names at the Chase was the Tenderloin Room. Some of the restaurants at the Chase came and went quickly, like the Sea Chase. Others, like the Chase Club, stayed for years. But the Tenderloin Room, which opened in March 1962, was the stalwart and the star.

It *felt* opulent—the red walls, the dark wood, the decorative features from a couple of demolished mansions on nearby Lindell Boulevard. It was located in the heart of the two buildings, off the corridor that connected what were originally two separate hotels, the Chase and the Park Plaza. There were no windows, adding to the feeling of security and seclusion.

While we thought of the Tenderloin Room as primarily a steakhouse until its recent update—its trademark dish is a pepperloin steak with a mustard-laden sauce—it wasn't always just meat and potatoes. The first chef, George J.P. Ferrand, a native of Monaco, chose for one of the signature dishes on the first menu a Spanish provincial specialty called *puchero*: various kinds of meat cooked with various vegetables, somewhere between a soup and a stew.

Wine with dinner? Of course. But a day after opening, a workman nudged a bottle with his elbow. The result was three hundred bottles of wine broken, worth an estimated $2,000 (in today's money about $17,000). Remarkably, the sommelier at the Tenderloin Room in its early years was not only young, but also a woman. Two years after the opening, twenty-six-year-old Patricia Hupperts was overseeing a cellar with 147 different wines.

The most fondly remembered employee has to be Henry "Hack" Ulrich, the maître d' who came from the Chase Club to open the Tenderloin Room. Hack was so much a legend that people who never were within miles of the hotel knew who he was. Listeners to the late-night programs from the Chase with Harry Fender, via KMOX, and viewers of the long-running *Wrestling at the Chase* television show from KPLR, whose studios were in the hotel, both heard casual mentions of Hack's name. His gift with VIPs and ordinary people made both feel at home. But rank does indeed have its privileges; Ulrich made sure his high-end regulars would get food delivered to their hospital rooms a few blocks south on Kingshighway. He was said to entertain very young guests by taking lobsters out of the tank and putting them to sleep by rubbing their bellies.

Another place Hack's name, and that of the restaurant, was heard was on Cardinals baseball broadcasts as announcers like Jack Buck discussed the players. Visiting teams stayed at the Chase, some players and managers lived on the high-rise Park Plaza side and after-game dining was common. Eagle-eyed youngsters occasionally were seen in the lobby waiting for a chance to beg for autographs as players and coaches headed for the team bus. Autograph-hunting, of course, occurred in other circumstances. Big-name musicians of the era played at the Chase Club and dined at the Tenderloin Room—the Sinatras and the Comos and the Belafontes. Elvis Presley stayed at the Chase but was hustled off to the freight elevators to avoid screaming fans. Movie stars did their press interviews there. Politicians wound down from campaigning over bourbon. Harry Truman was said to turn down fancy food and order a ham-and-cheese sandwich instead. Despite all the big names, it was a very discreet place from all reports. Maybe because it was dark, maybe because all eyes were on the glitterati, but lips were all but permanently sealed, even now, about some of the things, and people, seen there.

A fire in 1968 caused serious damage. The restaurant was moved to the lower level, where it was re-created within forty-eight hours and remained until the reopening of the original site in 1970. Hack retired in 1986, and the hotel itself closed in 1988, but the Tenderloin Room struggled on for another three years. Everyone agreed it was the end of an era.

Except that it wasn't. In 1999, a $100 million renovation led by Jim Smith and William Stallings brought the grande dame back to life. The Tenderloin

It's still elegant at the new Tenderloin Room.

Room was reopened by several members of the Karagiannis family, the first of whom had begun working there in 1963. The magic continued. George Clooney stayed at the Chase while filming *Up in the Air*, and the Karagiannises lost count after the actor's fortieth visit. He was, by all accounts, a seriously nice guy and engaged in a running discussion with staffers about their love lives, often offering advice. ("Honey, George Clooney told me we should.")

In 2019, there was another change in management. Ben Strake, Bob Brazell and Rick DeStefane, owners of Byrd & Barrel and Tamm Avenue Bar, took over. The menu and the look are updated. A snazzy bar menu is full of modern tastes as well as standards, and the cocktail offerings do the same; the dinner menu still offers the U.S. Senate bean soup and the pepperloin steak with a strong focus on red meat. The feel is sleek but still darkish and discreet.

The Tenderloin Room is just fine for the twenty-first century.

The Tenderloin Room
Chase Park Plaza Hotel
232 North Kingshighway Boulevard, St. Louis
314-361-0900
tenderloinroom.com

Tony's

T ony Bommarito opened Tony's Spaghetti House in 1946. It was a small place on what was then Produce Row between Broadway and Wharf Street, a tavern that he turned into a lunch spot for workers. He hadn't operated a restaurant before, but his father, Vincent, had a bakery, and his father-in-law had a factory that made pasta and sauce. An ad in 1947 announced,

    Spaghetti   *Meatballs*   *Chefs Salad*

He passed away only three years after opening it, leaving a widow and four children. The two boys were still at St. Louis University High School. Vincent, the eldest, was about to graduate. Mrs. Bommarito wanted the boys to go to college, but responsibility called Vince to go to work at the restaurant full time, and he did. His brother Anthony Jr., two years younger, felt the same way. They both graduated, and the place they'd been helping out at as kids soon became more or less theirs.

There they were, two young guys with a little restaurant. Both of them, but particularly Vince, were competitive. "How can we do it better?" became their mantra. Dinner hours were added. Tablecloths. Candles in Chianti bottles. New restrooms. An expanded kitchen. For a while, they even served breakfast. "We *tried*," recalled Vince. "If people weren't eating something, we tried adjusting it." Dinner, they found, was harder to get properly tuned than the businessmen's lunches.

It was a simple place, with linoleum floors, not the kind of spot for dressing up and dimming the lights. "But," said Vince, "we had an old Austrian man on the door, Mr. Leo, and he set the tone." Vince was a fast learner. "One night I heard him say to a customer, 'Is your steak done to your liking?'" Later, Vince asked Mr. Leo to repeat what he'd said. "Me, I was just asking them, 'Is your steak okay?'" Obviously, it was a case of when the student is ready, the teacher will come.

That kind of refined concern came to be the house standard. It was one reason why a 1955 story in the *St. Louis Globe-Democrat* explained to readers, "The place has none of the aspects of the neighborhood." It became something of a college hangout and one for artists as well; in 1951, a *Globe-Democrat* story discussed a gallery show of five artists who frequented the place, including a painting of the interior by an artist who'd moved to Miami. They decided in 1958 to concentrate solely on dinner.

But change was coming. During the 1950s, Produce Row had to move because of highways moving and bridge approaches. They took space at 826 Broadway at Franklin Avenue and eventually bought all the property at the southeast corner, razing four buildings and most of a fifth. What remained of that last building became a bar and lounge where patrons could wait to be seated; the rest of the lot served as parking for the restaurant. The dining rooms were adjacent to the bar on both the first and second floors.

Yes, the second floor, unusual in an American restaurant. But it gave the owners what was, for many years, literally their signature move. Vince didn't want his staff turning their backs on diners as they were led upstairs to their tables. So the maîtres d' walked backward up the stairs leading parties to be seated. They'd dropped the "Spaghetti House" phrase a while back, and there was a brief period as "Steak House." But by this time, the "House that Bommaritos Built" was on a first-name basis with the world. It had begun to emerge as what we would recognize today. It certainly was fine dining, and its national reputation began to glow fiercely. It became the only Italian restaurant in the United States to earn a Mobil five-star rating; the other eleven holders of the rank then were all French.

Vince Bommarito would say that much of the credit should go to his employees. He hired carefully, he trained thoroughly and he demanded that the high standards be maintained. The most notable among the employees had to have been maître d' Herb Cray. Elegant, unflappable, totally poised and equally able to deal with a bevy of senators or a couple of kids on a first visit before their prom, he presided over the dining room with a silken touch and, when appropriate, warmth. It would not have been difficult to imagine him running things at Buckingham Palace. Herb was there for more than thirty years.

That was not a record for length of employment, by any means. Other employees have been there forty, even fifty years. But another measure is of employees who left. In 1986, Vince was quoted as saying that at least two dozen of his former employees, mostly waiters, had opened their own restaurants. They include a great number of fine-dining destinations, most of them local.

The idea of making diners feel special was always part of the house game plan. When asked about how they seated people, Bommarito talked about maybe putting a young couple on a first date at the edge of the room so they wouldn't feel that people were staring at them; a table of businessmen with papers and drinks might go in the corner, out of the traffic. But, he added, "The peacocks go in the middle, with the other peacocks, so they can look at each other."

Once again, progress reared its ugly head. That particular corner of Broadway was being sucked up by urban development for an indoor stadium and convention center. The search was on again for a new site. In 1972, Anthony, the younger brother, had opened a French restaurant, Anthony's, at Broadway and Market in the Equitable Building. It closed in 1991. The following year, Tony's moved into that same space. The dining room was sleek and modern, but the staff still glided about, reading the body language of the diners, finishing dishes tableside on gueridons. By now, there were new Bommaritos on hand, including Vince's sons: Anthony; Vince Jr., who'd graduated from the Culinary Institute of America; and James. Anthony managed Anthony's Bar, in an adjacent space, which offered lunch in a smallish room reminiscent of the old Four Seasons in New York. Vinny, as young Vince was known, was not only in the kitchen

Sign outside the front door of Tony's.

but also sometimes in the front of the house. Previously, the kitchen staff was considered a team, and there was never much public play given to the concept of who led the kitchen. James, after playing linebacker at Rice University, worked the front of the house and became the cheese specialist.

Plenty of celebrities came to dine, of course, like sportscaster and former Cardinals catcher Tim McCarver, quietly eating alone and undisturbed at one side of the dining room. There were so many proposals done in the house that the restaurant lost count. Once, a young man brought an engagement ring to the staff on the day of his dinner reservation and asked to have it put into a glass of champagne to be served to his beloved. No one batted an eye at this sort of request, of course, and before dinner, two glasses of bubbly were brought forth. When they were emptied, they were removed—and then the man realized the woman hadn't seen the ring. The entire well-oiled kitchen came to a rapid, complete stop to search for the ring. It was indeed located, before the glass got to the dishwasher, and the evening proceeded. (She said "yes.")

The menu is high-scale comfort food, carefully cooked. Yes, pasta (there's a recipe for pasta primavera in the back of this book), but also superb soups and first courses. The signature entrée is lobster albanello. (Wise diners order some pasta to snuggle up to the sauce around the lobster.)

Even in an establishment like this, time causes changes. Anthony Bommarito, after closing Anthony's Bar in 1991, became a wine importer. Young Vince became the chief culinary officer for a catering company. And the patriarch, Vincent Bommarito Sr., passed away in April 2019. James Bommarito is now at the helm.

Over the years, the dress codes have relaxed and the style of food has evolved. Now more changes are ahead. They're about to trade the downtown location for one in Clayton. It'll be in Centene Centre C, on the east side of Brentwood between Forsyth and Carondelet. But Tony's will surely remain a marker of style and service and elegance to St. Louis.

Tony's
410 Market Street, St. Louis
314-231-7007
tonysstlouis.com

Trattoria Marcella

Trattoria Marcella is an excellent example of a restaurant that settled into a glowing middle age. That's no small achievement. The business is fraught with peril—un-tasty food, disappearing dishwashers, uncomfortable chairs. And don't laugh about those, because when they exist, people always complain about them, and you would, too.

Brothers Steve and Jamie Kormorek started with an edge. They have restaurants in their genes. Their mother, Marcella, was a member of the Slay family, who owned restaurants in town and who begat other Slays that became well known for their restauranting. Lisa cheffed for many years at Remy's Kitchen and Bar. David, who began in St. Louis with Cafe Hamton across from the family mother ship, opened several others and now is in Southern California with several restaurants and a winery. Those two are Steve and Jamie's cousins.

The Kormorek brothers began working in restaurants long before they could drive, and not just the family's operations. Steve mostly cooked; Jamie prefers working the front of the house and dealing with wine. Trattoria Marcella was conceived during an all-night drive back from Las Vegas sometime around 1990. They decided that instead of the French/Italian/Lebanese Mediterranean restaurant they'd been thinking about, they'd go for Italian food, but in a different way than most of what St. Louis had seen before. They opened in 1995.

Early on, a reviewer compared Trattoria Marcella (named, obviously, for the owners' mother) to similar places in Bologna. Bologna is known to

Italians as the second-best food city in Italy. (The best, of course, is whichever one the speaker grew up in. But Bologna is *almost* as good.) No hunks of meat with cheese melted on top, no pasta con broccoli. Real risotto, not rice with sauce stirred into it, as had been happening way too often in this town. The house fritto misto not only has calamari, it also has flash-fried spinach (a creation of their cousin David, by the way) and shards of Parmesan. Yes, *has*—present tense. It's remained on the menu since the establishment's opening, the sort of dish that makes people say, "I've got to stop eating this. I've got more food coming," and then reach for another bite. There are imaginative pastas and a potato gnocchi that should make one rise from a sickbed if it reappears on the changing menu. The kitchen understands pork as well as it does veal, and it has great respect for liver. Lobster risotto, a perpetual off-menu special, may be their trademark dish. The recipe is in the back of this book.

It certainly started out hot, one of the most in-demand restaurants in town. And it took a long time, more than the usual year or so, to cool down even a little. They quickly acquired regulars, both ordinary folks and the bold-faced names seen in newspaper columns. One guy who stopped in for a drink every evening told stories about that aviator "Charlie" Lindbergh. His favorite baseball player was Honus Wagner, whom he'd seen play. Business flourished; the space was enlarged from 60 seats to 100 in 1998, easing the ongoing crush. But that wasn't enough, and in 2004, an expansion to the rear brought the number up to 150. Things are a little easier now, and they've put in outside seating in front of the building.

Servers stay a long time, and customers mostly appreciate the good service. But still, there can be incidents. One night, a customer ordered beef tenderloin. When it arrived, he complained that it wasn't hot enough, although he'd not cut into it yet. The tenderloin was returned to the kitchen and warmed more. This time, he sliced into it and complained that it was overdone. They fired a whole new one and brought it out. The gent stared at it a moment and then announced, "Take it away. I don't want it." Jamie was well aware of what was going on and, indeed, had brought out the new one himself. "We pride ourselves on our service, and we've tried to give you what you wanted," he explained to the customer, "But your dinner check has been taken care of. We're going to ask you to leave now and not come back." The guy must have been making quite a scene, because the whole room applauded. He stalked out, taking his companion with him. But in a few minutes, he came in the door again. Jamie met him. And the man apologized, saying he'd had a really bad day.

How lovely to have a story like that with a pleasant ending.

There is now, literally, a sister restaurant, Marcella's Mia Sorella ("my sister") in Ballwin. It's not an identical twin, with similarities and the same management and attitude but with a somewhat different menu.

Between the expansions and time, it's now possible to walk in on weeknights and usually be seated straightaway, but calling first is always a good idea. Trattoria Marcella is having a very satisfying middle age.

Trattoria Marcella
3600 Watson Road, St. Louis
314-352-7706
trattoriamarcella.com

Uncle Bill's Pancake and Dinner House

Uncle Bill's Pancake and Dinner House on South Kingshighway may well be the only Tudor-style pancake house in the country. If it isn't, the customers who continue to pour through the doors don't care. The building itself is a sibling of the Cheshire Inn, by both looks and lineage, being the brainchild of William Medart, Cheshire's founder. Opened in 1932, it was a second location of his popular hamburger stand, a place you can find more details of in *Lost Restaurants of St. Louis*. He sold it in the 1940s to William and Bette Ernst.

The building housed a restaurant, DiFranco's, until 1959, when it became the Rizzo Brothers' Fireplace, which noted in its ads that it was serving Sunday breakfast. That only lasted until 1960, when the Ernsts renamed it Uncle Bill's Pancake House and Cocktail Lounge. They kept their liquor license, at least for a while, and had music in the lounge section. It's amusing to note that in 1964, several newspaper stories noted wedding breakfasts being held at Uncle Bill's Pancake House. (The receptions were held that same evening at another venue.) It's good to keep your strength up on the big day, but consider the difficulty of avoiding syrup on Chantilly lace and dainty fingertip veils, to cite the style of the time. Nevertheless, in the current day of receptions having doughnut "walls" and wedding cakes made of pies, one could imagine this fashion returning.

A fire in 1973 that started in the kitchen did considerable damage, and it took several months to reopen. Ernst moved things to a spot on Shaw Avenue, possibly 5046, where Guido's is now, but he returned when the

repairs and rebuilding were complete. The fireplace is still there, by the way, with a surround of blue-and-white tile.

The Ernsts sold the place in 1980, and there have been several owners since then. Two other locations were established, one at Lemay Ferry and Lindbergh, where Dohack's once was, which has closed, and another in Ballwin, which continues. The current owners are Richard Lee and William Choi.

Opposite: The fireplace at Uncle Bill's Pancake House, Kingshighway.

Left: Dining room at Uncle Bill's Pancake House, Kingshighway.

Despite the vaulted ceiling and brass chandeliers, it's a completely casual place, with a number of servers who have been there for years. The full range of humanity seems to come through these doors in the course of a year: families with babies, senior citizens, no-tie business meetings, post-club partiers, on and on. Interestingly, there's an automatic 15 percent gratuity tacked on to checks from 10:00 p.m. to 7:00 a.m. Perhaps the late-night folks are distracted from tipping by their companions. But then, of course, there are nights like the one in which limousines pulled up and deposited Bob Costas and fourteen pals after a big gala benefit soiree. Sadly, the glass display case by the entry no longer has for sale the ceramics that were hand-painted by the otherwise-anonymous Wanda. (Those Christmas trees with their wee lights are suddenly back in fashion. Like the pancake wedding breakfasts, ahead of their time?)

The surroundings should be a clue that this is not quite as inexpensive as, say, Waffle House, but there's no feeling of giving the bare minimum to customers. It's real half-and-half for the coffee; the bacon is thick and at the right stage between crisp and chewy; and the crepes are actually crepes, not just pancakes rolled up and given a new name. Yes, there are dinners, too, and sandwiches, although we suspect they're not nearly as popular as the breakfast chow.

Uncle Bill's is open twenty-four hours a day and on nearly all holidays, and they do take credit cards.

Uncle Bill's Pancake and Dinner House
3427 South Kingshighway, St. Louis
314-832-1973

14196 Manchester Road, Ballwin
636-394-1416

Union Station

If there's any structure that says "St. Louis" to the people who live here besides the Arch, it's Union Station. Theodore Link's massive-but-fanciful building combines Romanesque arches with the feel of a medieval French castle. It doesn't come to mind immediately, at least to most people, as a place to eat.

Certainly, its revival in 1985 by the Rouse Company of Baltimore gave us a number of restaurants, with interesting options. Lighthearted places like Tom Burnham's Key West Cafe stayed open late and hosted athletes and other well-known faces. (There was the night that Cathy Rigby, in town doing *Peter Pan*, was tossed from person to person by stagehands from the show.) The Big Red—the nickname of the football Cardinals before the Bidwill family uprooted them to the desert—alums Dan Dierdorf and Jim Hart opened their steakhouse along the Midway, one of the first tenants. It was so dark inside that one reviewer said that Grace Jones could be making out with John Ashcroft and no one would see them. The then-avant-garde Fedora is discussed in *Lost Restaurants of St. Louis*, with its modern American cuisine and its chef, Bill Cardwell, whose subsequent eponymous restaurant we talk about in this book.

But those are the easy ones. Long before those, more than ninety years before, in fact, other food was being served up in our station, the one that was grander than anything Chicago had for passenger trains. The dining room, as well as a casual sort of lunchroom and the newsstands, were all from the Fred Harvey Company. Yes, the restaurants that had the Harvey Girls.

Fred himself came to this country from England as a young man and ended up in St. Louis, where he became a naturalized citizen. Unfortunately, in 1861, through no fault of his own, his business here, a dining hall, failed. He moved to St. Joseph, Missouri, and started anew as a railroad agent. After a while, he began to travel through the West as part of his job. While trains stopped to take on fuel and water, passengers jumped off to quickly eat at the depot. The food and the settings were uniformly abysmal. Fred saw opportunity and began creating decent places to eat. He wanted a pleasant room, nice service and good food—no small order on the frontier.

In one way, he may have been as responsible for taming the West as the Wyatt Earps of his time. Setting up a system to get quality food delivered, getting the furniture and tableware for the dining rooms and establishing a written set of standards for the whole thing was a tremendous task. He was a demanding employer—he would drop in on a restaurant, and if things were not up to snuff, he would yank the tablecloth off a table to emphasize his dismay at the problems he encountered. He wanted a *civilized* experience for his customers.

By the time St. Louis was planning the grand station, Harvey had restaurants and several elegant hotels throughout the West as well as a long and profitable relationship with what became the Santa Fe Railroad. The Republican convention was to be held in St. Louis in 1896, two years after the projected opening of the St. Louis station, which meant even more attention to his work. He'd already teamed up with George Pullman to create luxury train cars with berths and dining cars, besides the hotels and restaurants in the West.

One of the tenets, Fred Harvey's Fundamentals, as he called them, was, "Remember, travel follows good food routes."

When he established his "eating houses," as he called them, one of the first things he insisted on was serving good coffee. That included making it fresh several times a day. He brought beef that was still pink inside to the western table. His servings of pie were almost a quarter of the pie. He hired serious chefs and gave them the tools to do first-rate work.

At St. Louis Union Station's opening on September 1, 1894, guests thronged the station, including the magnificent Grand Hall. There were two Harvey eateries, the dining room on the upper level, west of the Grand Hall, and a more casual place on the lower level, where his newsstand and other shops were located on the Midway, the area that opened onto the train platforms. The dining room in particular was elegantly done, with rich wood paneling and handsome light fixtures. Harvey had gone to Europe

The 1894 opening of the Grand Hall at St. Louis Union Station. *Courtesy of the National Museum of Transportation.*

to shop for Irish linen, Sheffield silver for his place settings, Limoges for his porcelains and Bordeaux for wines. That said, he was, in the wilder areas where he did business, happy to receive local game and fish for his kitchens.

One local product that Harvey used throughout his restaurants was the uniforms for his waitresses, known as the Harvey Girls. The Angelica Company, which began and remains in St. Louis, came into existence when the wife of a railroad dining-car chef, Cherubino Angelica, made him a white chef's jacket with a distinctive double-breasted style. It drew attention, and the Angelica family started making them, and other uniforms, including the Harvey Girls', commercially.

Because it served several different railroad companies (thus the name *Union*), the station saw many people passing through, not just St. Louisans arriving and departing. The wave of immigration from Europe was in full swing at the turn of the century, and many of those people headed farther west than the great port cities of the East. Farmland was available and alluring. Trains took them on into Oklahoma, Kansas and Colorado. One of the recipes in the back of this book was developed, it would appear, for such folks as the Russian Mennonites, one of many groups who passed through.

Everyone seemed to have something to eat at Fred Harvey's. In 1912, the former Democratic presidential candidate William Jennings Bryan had breakfast in the dining room with Joseph W. Folk, the former governor of Missouri and a progressive reformer. Breakfast and talks were so alluring, for whatever reason, that Bryan missed his train home. (Instead, he went to the

The main dining room of St. Louis Union Station in an undated photograph. *Courtesy of St. Louis Union Station.*

Terminal Hotel, had his pants pressed while he sat trouserless and then met with reporters at the Jefferson Hotel until the next train to Omaha.)

Union Station also became a destination for locals, as it would much later in the twentieth century. One family's habit was to have Sunday dinner there after church. Breakfast on New Year's Eve became a popular tradition. In the 1920s, it was big with college students. After games or movies, they would head to Harvey's for pancakes and then watch the late trains leave.

The baker for those restaurants then was a man named Harry Kelledy. His daughter reported that her father, an Irish American, was a baker by trade, but no one in those days would hire an Irish baker. Kelledy had attended a German elementary school and was quite fluent in the language. So, he changed the name on his application to Harry Mueller. He got the job and had a long career. There were German immigrants working in the bakery there who didn't speak English and who apparently never figured out that he wasn't German.

In the spring of 1941, the St. Louis Browns were the guests of honor at a "Welcome Home" breakfast in the dining room given by a group of fans called the Grandstand Managers and Grandstand Coaches. When the group repeated the event in 1943, the dining room was unavailable. The station was mobbed during World War II. Troops were in transit, gasoline and tires were rationed and trains were invariably crowded. The upstairs dining room was turned into a USO operation, the vintage light fixtures traded out for fluorescent tubes. Nevertheless, the attempts at normalcy were valiant, and the Brownies' homecoming breakfast went forward.

One passenger traveling via St. Louis Union Station was a fellow from Independence, Missouri. Harry S Truman had been elected to the Senate in 1934, and his general method of transportation between Independence and Washington, D.C., was via railroad. He enjoyed the food at Harvey restaurants and said so publicly, although he was generally a ham sandwich sort of guy by his own admission. He was, however, very fond of their Wisconsin cheese soup, and we have that recipe in the back. Truman had to change trains in St. Louis each time. That was how the famous photograph of President Truman gleefully holding up a two-day-old copy of the *Chicago Daily Tribune* with its infamously inaccurate headline "DEWEY DEFEATS TRUMAN" was taken in St. Louis Union Station in 1948. He was on his way back to work after voting in his beloved Independence.

The postwar years were disastrous for passenger train travel. Commercial airlines thrived, and their cost came down. The interstate highway system

The main dining room today, now known as the Station Grille.

began to make auto travel faster and easier, if considerably less interesting. All over the country, train stations fell into a slumber or closed entirely. At Union Station, the upstairs dining room closed by 1960, although it was used for special events under the name the Louis IX Room, with a portable dance floor sometimes placed in the middle.

Eventually, though, it was time to find the chloroform. Only four passenger trains a day were leaving the station, and on October 31, 1978, the last train left. For several years before that, one could almost feel the ghosts about. The local Theatre Project Company had been using the ladies' waiting room east of the Grand Hall for its work, and by the end it was very strange, indeed, said attendees.

But the rebirth in 1985 and the recent rejuvenation have brought new life to the historic spot. The Hilton Hotel Curio Collection now runs the main building. The dining room is called the Station Grille. And now, finally, one can eat in the glorious Grand Hall, which is also home to a sound and light show. In addition, there are two new restaurants in the train yard, the Soda Fountain and the Train Shed, in addition to Landry's Seafood House and the coming 1894 Cafe.

Whatever ghosts there are, or were, were certainly well fed.

Union Station
1820 Market Street, St. Louis
www.stlouisunionstation.com

Velvet Freeze

Baskin Robbins? 1945. Swensen's? 1948. Häagen-Dazs? 1961, for crying out loud.

Velvet Freeze was there before them. It began in 1935, "down on the Gravois," as the old Southsiders used to say. The Grosberg brothers made ice cream cones, quite a lot of them, it appears. They were Russian émigrés, and so was Jacob Martin, who had ice cream stores. They decided to merge, using the name of Martin's ice cream, Velvet Freeze. Martin already had eleven stores; expansion followed rapidly, despite the Depression, and within a few years, there were fifty. Eventually, they expanded to Kansas City, where, at one time, there were twenty stores, and several locations in Illinois and Wisconsin.

For a world mostly used to the options of vanilla, chocolate or strawberry ice cream, it must have been mind-blowing to see the variety of flavors compared to the fountain at the corner drugstore. In the prime years of the company, there were always thirty basic flavors in stock, and another ten were seasonal, rotating through the year. Perhaps the most well remembered is the Gold Coast Chocolate, very dark indeed, and woe betide the white shirt that got drips of Gold Coast on it. Swiss chocolate was not a milder, milkier chocolate, but a chocolate chip variation. Peach was a summertime favorite. Butter pecan sold well, and so did black walnut, the earthy flavor so beloved by some midwesterners. Of course, there was peppermint, just waiting for some hot fudge to be ladled over it. Sundaes, ice cream sodas (so

The Velvet Freeze ice cream cone outside Mesnier Primary School in Affton, originally at the Velvet Freeze Store located at Gravois and Weber Road.

difficult to find these days), shakes, malts and banana splits—all were handed across the counters.

There were fountain sodas, of course. In addition, some of the stores had a grill for hamburgers and such. But most went no further than a small electric oven to heat packaged sandwiches from Landshire, including a sort of hero called a Nike, named, presumably, for the antiaircraft missile. Everything was self-service, with a few slide-in plastic booths, a line of chairs and a wall of glass-doored freezer cases for bulk ice cream and other dairy products. During holidays, there were bricks of ice cream that, when sliced, revealed Christmas trees or Easter rabbits. The aroma was always of sugar and vanilla, occasionally punctuated by the passing whiff of one of the sandwiches being unwrapped in a small cloud of steam.

After-church traffic, after-school traffic, after–Little League traffic, all came and went. At least one store posted a "Teen Time 15 minutes" sign near its clock, but it didn't seem vigorously enforced. The rowdy crowds always seemed to respect the sparkling, sweet-scented stores and do their mischief elsewhere.

Pizza and fast food began to flourish, and perhaps that heralded the beginning of the end for most of the Velvet Freeze stores. At this writing, there's one left, at 7355 West Florissant Road in Jennings, and it's making its ice cream in the back of the store. Many of the nostalgic flavors have been re-created by nostalgic St. Louisan Beckie Jacobs at her store, Serendipity Ice Cream, 8130 Big Bend Boulevard in Webster Groves. And, yes, there's definitely Gold Coast Chocolate.

Woofie's Hot Dogs

St. Louis is not a hot dog town, not the way Chicago or New York is (despite the latter's awful habit of cooking onions before they go onto the dog). And it's not at all one like Tucson, with its amazing Sonoran hot dogs.

And yet Woofie's has persisted. Loyal fans say there's nothing like it. There's certainly nothing like it for nearly as long. In 1976, Charlie Eisen and partners bought a property that had been Hamburger Heaven on Woodson Road in Overland. He, Herman Fishman and son Steve and Harold Schilling opened in February 1977. Eisen, who'd had a pawnshop in Jennings, wanted something new. Fishman was a distributor for Vienna Beef hot dogs, the highly regarded all-beef dog so deeply embedded in the Chicago tradition. Charlie was the face of the business, though, the guy who was there every day. His wife, Marilyn, was there nearly as often.

Eisen used to describe the place as postage-stamp sized. It's not quite that small, but there are perhaps a dozen stools inside pulled up to counters. The drill is as follows: order at the cash register and pick up your order a yard to the right at another opening in the glass. A lot of the business is to-go. After a few years, they put in a drive-through window, then an awning and some concrete picnic tables and benches. That means there are not many people waiting, hot dogs in hand, for other diners to finish up. Celebrity photos, mostly local, come and go on the walls, according to some secret protocol. Aside from the occasional paint job and a new crop of petunias every year, things haven't changed much in forty-plus years.

Woofie's, a little larger than a postage stamp.

For a while, there was a location at Clayton and Woods Mill and another in the Jewish Community Center. Those closed, and others opened on West Florissant and at Dorsett and Fee Fee Roads. Those, too, eventually disappeared. But the mother ship carries on.

Many variations on the hot dog are on the menu, but the best seller is still the Woofie, a classic Chicago dog, steamed on a poppy seed bun, topped with mustard, onion, evil green relish (to use a reviewer's phrase), a tomato wedge and a couple of sport peppers (small pickled peppers of medium heat and vinegary tartness). Never ketchup. (It's available on the counters with the napkins.) Fries come showered with seasoned salt, not unlike Lawry's. Also available are corn dogs, Polish, larger hot dogs and some hamburgers, although it's rare to see them ordered.

Stories about Woofie's abound. A Cardinals rainout ended up with Bob Costas and Dan Dierdorf doing a call-in show from the stand. With only one phone in the place, Costas, whose idea it was in the first place, stayed inside, and Dierdorf was relegated to his car phone. Police had to be called to direct traffic when people realized where they were. Another time, a woman went into labor just as she got her order during lunch hour. Charlie called 911, but the woman did get to finish her hot dog.

Charlie Eisen died in 1997. The business was sold to Paul and JoAnn Fitzgerald, who lived nearby. Things perked along, and Woofie's was given admission to the Vienna Beef Hot Dog Hall of Fame. Paul sold Woofie's in 2017 to Craig Smith and his wife, Mary O'Leary.

It all continues. In January 2020, Woofie's sold its one millionth hot dog. That's ninety-four miles of hot dogs. Charlie Eisen used the slogan "Serving the hot dog with dignity." And so they have. It's an institution. And, by the way, don't be put off by the address on the door. It says 1919 *Woofson* Road. Could be, could be....

Woofie's Hot Dogs
1919 Woodson Road, Overland
314-426-6291
woofiesstl.com

PART II

RECIPES FROM ST. LOUIS RESTAURANTS

Annie Gunn's Roquefort Potato Casserole

This potato dish is basically a variation on potatoes au gratin. It's often made with other kinds of bleu cheese from the Smoke House Market next door to Annie Gunn's. Definitely a very rich dish of gooey goodness, it will stand up to almost any roast meat. Yes, it's a generous amount of black pepper, but this is quite a lot of potatoes. It all balances out nicely.

5 medium Idaho potatoes (about 2 pounds)
¾ cup plain dried breadcrumbs, divided
10 ounces Roquefort cheese, crumbled
½ cup freshly grated Parmigiano-Reggiano cheese
2 tablespoons ground black pepper
1 cup heavy cream

Peel and boil potatoes until almost tender. Do not overcook. Let cool, then slice thinly the long way.

Preheat oven to 350 degrees. Grease a shallow 8-by-8-inch pan. Layer a fourth of the potatoes in the pan. Top with ¼ cup breadcrumbs, a fourth of the Roquefort, a fourth of the Parmigiano and 2 teaspoons of the pepper. Pour ⅓ cup cream over the top. Repeat the layers twice, and finish with the potatoes and the cheeses.

Cover pan with foil and bake for 20 minutes. Remove foil and bake until browned on top, another 10–15 minutes. Remove from oven and let cool at least 10 minutes as potatoes absorb the last of the liquid and firm up.

Serves 6.

Cardwell's Chinese Barbecue Chicken Salad

Sometimes, wonton sheets can be found pre-fried, as squares or strips.
They can be substituted here, crumbling the squares.

12 wonton sheets
About 2 cups vegetable oil for frying
4 chicken breast halves (about 6 or 7 ounces each)
4 cups shredded iceberg lettuce
2 cups shredded red cabbage
2 large carrots, grated
1 ½ cups peanut dressing (see recipe)
2 teaspoons sesame seeds
¼ cup roasted peanuts

Cut wonton sheets into strips ¼-inch wide. Deep fry or pan fry in vegetable oil until crisp. Drain. (You can make the fried wontons up to 1 day in advance.) Grill or broil chicken breasts about 8 minutes a side, until texture is firm and inside is not pink. Cut into strips and set aside. Combine lettuce, cabbage, carrots and chicken strips. Toss with dressing. Garnish with sesame seeds, roasted peanuts and wonton strips.

Yields 4 large servings.

Peanut Dressing
½ cup soy sauce
¼ cup rice wine vinegar
¼ cup vegetable oil
¼ cup dark (toasted) sesame oil
¼ cup granulated sugar
¼ cup hoisin sauce
1 teaspoon chili garlic sauce
1 tablespoon minced fresh ginger
¾ cup plus 2 tablespoon smooth peanut butter, divided
¼ teaspoon minced fresh mint leaves
1 teaspoon minced fresh cilantro

Mix together soy sauce, rice wine vinegar, vegetable oil, dark sesame oil, sugar, hoisin sauce, chili garlic sauce and ginger. Put half the peanut butter into a food processor and combine with half the liquid. Process until smooth. Scrape into a bowl.

Repeat with the rest of the peanut butter and of the liquid. Combine the two batches. Stir in the mint and cilantro. Leftover dressing may be refrigerated.

Yields 2½ cups.

The Crossing's Bleu Cheese Souffle

The Crossing has served an individual ramekin of this to every table since it opened. It arrives warm and creamy with pieces of bread for spreading. The Crossing serves it in ramekins that hold 3–4 ounces. Here we've got a larger version, nice for putting out with crostini to go with drinks before dinner.

1 egg, lightly beaten
¼ cup milk
1 cup mayonnaise
1 cup finely crumbled bleu cheese
1 cup diced onion
¼ teaspoon salt or to taste
¼ teaspoon ground pepper or to taste

Preheat oven to 300 degrees. Stir together egg, milk, mayonnaise, cheese, onion, salt and pepper. Transfer to an 8-inch square glass or ceramic baking dish. Place the baking dish in a larger roasting pan and place in the oven. Then pour hot water into the roasting pan until it's about halfway up the sides of the baking dish. Bake 45 minutes or until the souffle is set on top and lightly browned.

Serve hot with crusty bread or crackers.

Serves about 16.

The Forum Cafeteria's Chicken Pot Pie

The Forum was known for having a fine hand with fowl. Here's the chicken pot pie recipe. You're on your own for the crust, and we won't tell if you use frozen or a mix.

Pie dough, already prepared
1 egg
1 tablespoon water
⅓ cup chicken fat (originally used) or vegetable oil
⅓ cup flour
3½ cups chicken stock or low-sodium canned broth
3 drops yellow food coloring
1 teaspoon salt or less, to taste
1 pinch ground white pepper
2 cups diced cooked potatoes
¼ cup frozen peas
2½ cups cooked chicken, cut into ¾-inch-wide strips

Preheat oven to 425 degrees.

Roll pie dough out to ⅛-inch thickness. If you are making individual casseroles, cut the dough to the size and shape of each dish. If you are serving the pot pie in one large casserole, cut one piece of dough.

Place dough on cookie sheets. Prick with fork to prevent excessive puffing or blistering.

Beat egg with water to make an egg wash. Brush on top of dough. (You will not need all the egg wash.) Bake 15 minutes until golden brown. Set aside.

In a saucepan, combine the chicken fat or oil and the flour. Cook over low heat, stirring constantly, until mixture turns a light golden brown about 10–15 minutes. Meanwhile, bring the stock to a boil. Stir in food coloring, salt and pepper. Slowly add the stock to the roux created by the fat and flour, stirring all the while. (Be careful; stock will sputter and boil furiously.) With a whisk, keep stirring to make a smooth gravy. Stir in the potatoes, peas and chicken; heat through.

Divide among the individual casseroles or the large dish. Cover with pastry and serve.

Serves 4.

Charlie Gitto's On the Hill's Penne Borghese

¼ cup extra-virgin olive oil
½ cup finely diced yellow onion
I cup finely diced prosciutto (about 6 ounces)
½ cup chopped fresh parsley
¼ cup cognac or brandy
I cup tomato sauce
3 cups heavy cream
¼ teaspoon salt or to taste
⅛ teaspoon ground black pepper or to taste
I pound penne, cooked and drained
½ cup freshly grated Parmigiano cheese, for garnish.

Heat oil in a large sauté pan or Dutch oven; add onion, prosciutto and parsley. Cook until onion is translucent, about 2 minutes.

Remove the pan from the heat. Add cognac or brandy, scraping the bottom of the pan with a wooden spoon to loosen any brown bits. Return the pan to the heat.

Add the tomato sauce and cream, stirring until well incorporated. Cook to reduce slightly. Add salt and pepper. Add cooked penne; simmer, tossing, until pasta is hot and thoroughly coated. Pour onto a platter and serve immediately, garnished with Parmigiano.

Serves 4, about 10 cups.

Kemoll's Petto Di Pollo All'agro Dolce

2 skinless, boneless chicken breast halves
About ¼ cup all-purpose flour
¼ cup clarified butter (see note)
¼ cup plus 2 tablespoons wine vinegar
¼ cup plus 2 tablespoons water

2 teaspoons capers
2 tablespoons golden raisins
¼ cup plus 1 tablespoon granulated sugar
2 tablespoons chopped whole almonds, toasted

Pound chicken to an even thickness of about ⅜ inch; dip in flour and shake off excess. Heat a skillet over medium-high heat. Add butter and chicken. Brown both sides of chicken, turning only once. Remove chicken, set aside and keep warm.

Add vinegar, water, capers, raisins and sugar to the skillet; place over high heat and stir to combine. Cook one or two minutes until sauce is reduced and slightly thickened. Stir in almonds. Return chicken to skillet, including any juices that accumulate. Cook until chicken is done, about 3 minutes.

Place chicken on serving plates, pour sauce over.

Serves 2.

Note: To clarify butter, melt 1 stick butter. Cool, then chill. Lift off solids and discard white liquid. Melt the solidified butterfat again for easy measuring.

Mai Lee's Stir-Fried Vegetables in Sate Sauce

Sate sauce, sometimes spelled "satay," is a peanut-based sauce. Qui Tran of Mai Lee uses a brand called Yeo's. Sate sauce can be bought at Asian groceries and at least one of the major St. Louis grocery chains.

½ small onion, cut in 1-inch pieces
½ medium carrot, sliced
1 cup coarsely chopped cabbage (about ⅛ head)
1 cup broccoli florets
½ green bell pepper, cut in 1-inch pieces
1 tablespoon vegetable oil
1 clove garlic, minced
2 tablespoons minced lemongrass (use tender inner portion of the bottom of the stalk)

2½ tablespoons soy sauce
2–3 tablespoons sate sauce
1 tablespoon granulated sugar
4 mushrooms, sliced
¼ cup bamboo shoots
¼ cup sliced water chestnuts
8–10 snow peas, strings removed
Tops of 2 green onions, cut in 1½-inch pieces

Bring water to a boil in medium saucepan. Add onion, carrot, cabbage, broccoli and bell pepper. Cook until vegetables begin to soften, about 4 minutes. Drain and set aside.

Heat wok or stir-fry pan over medium high heat. Add oil and then garlic. Cook until garlic begins to brown. Add lemongrass. Stir in soy sauce and sate sauce. Add sugar; mix well.

Add drained cooked vegetables, then mushrooms, bamboo shoots, water chestnuts, snow peas and green onions. Stir fry until crisp-tender, 1½ to 3 minutes.

Serves 2–3.

Pope's Cafeteria's Nut Torte

This recipe was so popular that it was printed at least three times over the years in the *St. Louis Post-Dispatch*. Traditionally, it was made with bananas, but one can imagine fresh peaches or strawberries in it instead. The "all-purpose vegetable shortening" referred to is one like Crisco.

All-purpose vegetable shortening
½ cup white sugar
½ cup firmly packed brown sugar
½ cup plus 2 tablespoons graham cracker crumbs
½ cup chopped pecans
4 egg whites, room temperature
⅛ teaspoon cream of tartar
½ teaspoon vanilla

½ teaspoon almond flavoring
1 large banana, sliced
2 cups whipped cream
Garnish: maraschino cherries, slivered almonds or pecan pieces

Preheat oven to 300 degrees. Generously grease an 8-by-2-inch round baking pan well with shortening. Sift together the white sugar and brown sugar and set aside. In another container, combine graham cracker crumbs and pecans and set aside.

Place the egg whites and the cream of tartar in a large mixing bowl. Beat until the egg whites form soft peaks. Add sugars gradually, beating after each addition, until sugars are well incorporated into the egg whites. After all the sugar has been added, continue beating for another 5 minutes or until the egg whites are glossy and stand in stiff peaks. Add vanilla and almond flavoring, mix in thoroughly.

Sprinkle a third of the crumb-pecan mixture over the egg whites and fold in very gently. Gradually add remaining mixture, folding gently after each addition.

Gently pour the batter into the prepared pan. Bake for about 30 minutes, until the top of the torte is firm to the touch but still light in color. Remove from the oven.

Let cool in the pan and then remove to serving plate. (Some report that removing it after 15 minutes creates less sticking to the pan.) Slice banana over the top of the torte, cover with the whipped cream and sprinkle with the nuts and cherries. Refrigerate until ready to serve.

Serves 8–12.

Rizzo's Top of the Tower Salad Dressing

3 ounces cream cheese, softened
3 ounces bleu cheese, crumbled
6 tablespoons water
1 raw egg or ½ cup egg substitute
4½ teaspoons lemon juice
1 cup vegetable oil, divided

¼ cup red wine vinegar
¼ teaspoon prepared mustard such as French's
¾ teaspoon paprika
¾ teaspoon sea salt
¼ teaspoon garlic powder
½ teaspoon white pepper
1 tablespoon sugar
2 teaspoons snipped chives
1–2 tablespoons prepared horseradish
1½ teaspoons Worcestershire sauce
6 cups torn iceberg lettuce leaves
3½ cups torn romaine lettuce leaves
1 cup endive leaves
1 hard-boiled egg, chopped
Seasoned salt, such as Lawry's, to taste
Ground black pepper, to taste
Anchovy fillets (optional)

Combine cream cheese and bleu cheese and beat until smooth. Gradually add water to cheese mix until it is a pouring consistency.

Place raw egg or egg substitute, lemon juice and ¼ cup vegetable oil in blender and blend at medium speed for 15 seconds. Slowly increase speed and gradually add remaining ¾ cup of vegetable oil. Add vinegar, mustard, paprika, sea salt, garlic powder, white pepper, sugar, chives, horseradish and Worcestershire sauce and blend until smooth.

In a large salad bowl, mix iceberg, romaine and endive. Pour in enough of cheese dressing and oil dressing to coat greens. Sprinkle with chopped egg, seasoned salt and black pepper to taste. Toss gently three times.

Garnish with anchovy if desired.

Schlafly Tap Room's Sticky Toffee Pudding

This is the American version of Sheena Kopman's original recipe and, like many recipes from the United Kingdom and Europe, uses weight rather than volume for dry measure. You can look up equivalent volumes, which is to say cups or fractions of a cup, of sugar and flour on the internet. Chopping dates is most easily done by greasing the blade of a knife or kitchen scissors.

1 pound (16 ounces) chopped dried dates
2 cups hot water
2 teaspoons baking soda
5 ounces (10 tablespoons) unsalted butter, room temperature
1 pound sugar
5 eggs, room temperature
1 pound flour
2 teaspoons baking powder
Pinch of salt
2 teaspoons vanilla
Toffee sauce (recipe follows)
Whipped cream

Combine dates and hot water in a saucepan. Bring to a boil. Remove from heat; add baking soda. Set aside to cool.

Grease and flour a 9-by-13-inch pan. Preheat oven to 350 degrees.

Cream butter and sugar on high speed in an electric mixer for about 3 minutes, until pale and fluffy. Slow mixer to lowest speed, add eggs one at a time, beating after each addition and scraping bowl as necessary. When mixture is well combined, add flour, baking powder and salt. Add dates and their liquid, then vanilla, stirring just enough to combine everything evenly.

Pour into prepared pan and bake 25–30 minutes. A toothpick or skewer inserted in the middle should come out clean. Allow cake to cook before removing it from pan.

Toffee Sauce

4 packed cups dark brown sugar
1 pound butter
2 teaspoons vanilla
1 cup heavy cream

In a heavy saucepan over low heat, stir together sugar, butter and vanilla until butter melts. Raise heat to medium and continue to cook and stir until sugar dissolves. Remove from heat and whisk in the cream.

Squares of cake can be warmed in the microwave. The sauce should be warm to hot before it's ladled over pieces of cake, and please do not forget some whipped cream!

Makes about 18 squares.

Sidney Street Cafe's Caramelized Onion Tart

Chef Kevin Nashan, a great believer in local products, prefers to use Baetje Farms goat cheese, from Bloomsdale, Missouri. If it's not available, another goat cheese may be substituted.

Five separate preparations are called for to make this appetizer, which makes it an example of why it's not only the cost of ingredients at fine-dining restaurants, it's also the cost and knowledge of personnel. The recipe is, to a certain degree, in chef-speak, and in some cases the amount of an ingredient is not specified. But it's interesting to see what has to happen to put that tart on the table in front of a diner.

Onion Tart Filling
Oil, for sautéing
2 yellow onions, sliced
9 ounces Baetje goat cheese
3 ounces triple crème cheese
1 lemon, zested

Heat the oil in a medium saucepan over medium-high heat. Add the onions and cook to caramelize to a dark brown color.

In the top of a double boiler over simmering water, melt the two cheeses into a smooth mixture. Fold in the onions and the lemon zest.

Pearl Onion Preparation
Water
4 tablespoons butter
8 ounces red and white pearl onions
Thyme
Salt

In a medium saucepan set over medium-high heat, add some water and slowly whisk in the butter to form an emulsion. Add the onions and cook until tender, watching the braise; if it starts to break, add some water to bring it back together. Season with thyme and salt. Let cool for 4 minutes.

Cippolini Onion Caramelization
Dash of oil
8 ounces cippolini onions
Dash of sherry vinegar
Dash of water
Butter
Honey

In a sauté pan set over medium heat, add the oil and the onions. Caramelize the onions completely, then add a splash each of sherry vinegar and water. Make sure the mixture coats the onions, then reduce the heat to low.

Green Onion Puree
12 green onion tops
1 cup spinach
2 tablespoons vegetable oil
Salt

Bring a pot of water to a boil and prepare an ice bath. Blanch the onion tops and the spinach and then shock in the prepared ice bath. Wring out all the water and pat dry on a towel. Place the greens in a mixer with a tablespoon of oil; start to blend. Once the mixture starts to incorporate, continue adding the remaining tablespoon of oil and mix until it forms a smooth puree. Season with salt and let cool.

Pie Crust
3 cups all-purpose flour
3 tablespoons powdered sugar
8 ounces frozen butter, cubed
4 ounces cold water

In a food processor, place the flour, sugar and butter. Start to mix. Once the butter is cut into the flour, slowly add the ice water until it forms a grainy dough. Remove from the mixer and knead until it forms a ball. Rest for 30 minutes before rolling out.

Parmigiano-Reggiano for topping
Preheat the oven to 325 degrees.

Roll out the dough to ⅛-inch thickness and cut into desired mold shape. Bake whatever size tart shells you choose for 20 minutes. When the tart shells cool, fill each shell with the filling. Grate some cheese over each tart, return to the oven and bake until hot. Pull out of the oven and serve with the green onion puree, the caramelized cippolinis and the pearl onions as desired.

Serves 8.

Sweetie Pie's Macaroni and Cheese

Forget the stuff in a box. This is definitely the cheesiest.

1 pound (16 ounces) elbow macaroni
1 cup whole milk
2 12-ounce cans evaporated milk
3 eggs
2 sticks (8 ounces, or 1 cup) butter, cut into small pieces
½ pound Colby cheese, shredded
½ pound Monterey Jack cheese, shredded
½ pound sharp cheddar cheese
1 pound Velveeta cheese, cut in small chunks
Salt, to taste
1 tablespoon white pepper
1 tablespoon Sugar
1 cup shredded American or mild cheddar cheese

Preheat oven to 350 degrees. Bring a large pot of lightly salted water to a boil. Cook pasta according to package directions. Drain the pasta and transfer it to a 9-by-13-inch casserole dish. Set aside.

In a large bowl, combine the whole milk, evaporated milk and eggs. Mix with a fork until thoroughly combined.

Add the butter and Colby, Monterey Jack, sharp cheddar and Velveeta cheeses to the pasta.

Pour the milk and egg mixture over the pasta. Add salt, pepper and sugar and toss. Sprinkle the top of the pasta with the American or mild cheddar cheese.

Bake for 30–45 minutes, until the top is lightly browned.

Serves 10.

Tony's Pasta Primavera (Capelli D'Angelo, Primavera)

This seemingly simple pasta dish was all the rage when it hit Le Cirque back in the days of Truman Capote and his "swans," the beautiful socialites he knew. It remains a reliable vegetarian standby, light and satisfying. The vegetables can be adjusted as desired, but remember that *primavera* means "spring," and it was originally intended to use new, young spring vegetables.

Angel-hair pasta is very thin and is often sold coiled into nests. Because it is so thin, it is very easy to overcook, so watch it carefully.

¾ cup finely chopped assorted vegetables (asparagus, broccoli, cauliflower, zucchini and/or mushrooms)
1 nest of uncooked angel-hair pasta
3 tablespoons butter
Salt and pepper to taste

Fill a 3- or 4-quart pot with water; add vegetables. Bring to a boil. Add pasta to the water and cook until pasta is about three-fourths done. (Follow package directions or test it, or both.) Drain off most but not all of the water. Add butter to the mixture in the pot, stir well and continue cooking until pasta is al dente. (The butter combines with the starch to make a sort of sauce that coats the pasta, which is flavored by cooking it with the vegetables.)

Add salt and pepper to taste

Yields 1 generous serving.

Trattoria Marcella's Lobster Risotto

Steve Kormorek explains that a 1-pound lobster will give about 1 ¼ cups of meat when it's picked out from the flesh. Either steam it yourself or buy one already cooked. Save the shell and other debris to make the stock. Steve says to drop the shell and debris into boiling water with a chopped onion, a chopped bulb of fennel and a few black peppercorns and simmer for about 30 minutes. Strain before using. Or you could use clam juice, diluted.

Arborio rice is easier to find in grocery stores these days, but it's always available at the grocery stores on The Hill or at Global Foods in Kirkwood. This technique differs a little from the classic, but the results are delicious.

4 ½ cups lobster stock
2 teaspoons extra-virgin olive oil
¼ cup finely diced onion
½ cup sliced assorted mushrooms, such as crimini, shiitake and oyster
½ teaspoon minced garlic
½ cup dry white wine
1 cup arborio rice
½ cup tomato sauce
1 cup cooked lobster meat, cut in small bites
1 cup fresh spinach leaves
½ cup grated Parmigiano cheese
Salt
Ground white pepper to taste

Bring stock just to a simmer in a saucepan. Keep hot.

Heat olive oil in a large, thick-bottomed pan like a Dutch oven or deep skillet. Add onion and sauté gently until translucent. Add butter and mushrooms, cook over medium heat until mushrooms are soft. Add the garlic and cook just until it starts to brown.

Stir in wine. Cook until it's reduced by half.

Add rice, tomato sauce and 1 cup stock. Cook, stirring often. Add remaining stock about ½ cup at a time, waiting until each addition is fully absorbed before adding the next. Cook until rice is al dente, soft on the outside but very slightly firm inside.

Remove from the heat. Stir in the lobster meat, spinach and cheese. Allow the heat to soften the spinach. Season to taste with salt and pepper and serve immediately.

Serves 4 as a first course.

Fred Harvey's Cream of Wisconsin Cheese Soup

This was said to be a favorite of Harry Truman's, which he ate at St. Louis's Union Station and later at Union Station in Kansas City.

Place 12 saltine crackers in oven to warm. In a saucepan, heat 2 cups of beef broth over medium heat. Add 3 cups grated sharp cheddar cheese, stirring constantly as it melts. Add remaining quart of beef broth and simmer until smooth. Meanwhile, in a small skillet over medium heat, make a roux with 3 tablespoons butter and 3 tablespoons all-purpose flour. When smooth, add to first mixture. Continue stirring as you slowly add 1 cup light cream, 1 tablespoon Worcestershire sauce and ¼ teaspoon white pepper. Stir constantly at simmer for 15 minutes. Serve with toasted crackers.

Fred Harvey's Cauliflower Greens Restelli

This was created by a sous-chef at St. Louis Union Station for the droves of new immigrants passing through.

Sauté 2 tablespoons chopped onion and three strips of bacon, diced, in 2 teaspoons of olive oil until tender but not brown. Add ½ cup chopped tomatoes, ½ cup tomato puree and ½ clove garlic, minced. Wash 1 cauliflower (1¼ pounds), including the good leaves and stems, chop fine. Cook 5 minutes in boiling salted water and drain. Add to tomato sauce and serve. Sprinkle grated Parmesan cheese over each serving if desired.

Index

About the Author

Ann Lemons Pollack has been writing about food a good while, but not so long that she remembers all the restaurants in this book. She's reviewed restaurants, written cooking columns, traveled for food and was daring enough to cook for and then marry the restaurant critic of the *St. Louis Post-Dispatch*, Joe Pollack. Together, they wrote three guidebooks to St. Louis food and many food and travel stories. Ann carries on the tradition and is currently found monthly in and online at *St. Louis Magazine* and on her blog, stlouiseats.typepad.com, where she also writes about theater.